Edward T. Cook

Studies in Ruskin

Some Aspects of the Work and Teaching of John Ruskin. Second Edition

Edward T. Cook

Studies in Ruskin
Some Aspects of the Work and Teaching of John Ruskin. Second Edition

ISBN/EAN: 9783337001711

Printed in Europe, USA, Canada, Australia, Japan

Cover: Foto ©Thomas Meinert / pixelio.de

More available books at **www.hansebooks.com**

STUDIES IN RUSKIN.

SOME ASPECTS

OF THE

WORK AND TEACHING OF JOHN RUSKIN.

𝔅𝔞𝔩𝔩𝔞𝔫𝔱𝔶𝔫𝔢 𝔓𝔯𝔢𝔰𝔰
BALLANTYNE, HANSON AND CO.
EDINBURGH AND LONDON

STUDIES IN RUSKIN:

SOME ASPECTS

OF THE

WORK AND TEACHING OF JOHN RUSKIN.

BY

EDWARD T. COOK, M.A.,

AUTHOR OF

. "A POPULAR HANDBOOK TO THE NATIONAL GALLERY."

SECOND EDITION.

GEORGE ALLEN,

SUNNYSIDE, ORPINGTON,

AND

8, BELL YARD, TEMPLE BAR, LONDON.

1891.

First Edition printed 1890.
Second Edition printed 1891.

PREFACE.

THE object of the First Part of this little book is not, it will be seen, critical or controversial, but expository. My desire has been to discuss not *how*, but *what*, Ruskin has written. For several reasons, such definition seemed to me a thing worth attempting at this time. Mr. Ruskin has of late years written so voluminously, and on subjects so multifarious, that the accidental and the temporary have been like to overlay what is essential and permanent in his teaching. His writings open a vista into a great forest, but there has been some danger of not seeing the forest for the trees. This danger, which always exists when an author spreads himself over a large area, has probably been increased by the increasing popularity of Mr. Ruskin's

works, and by the cult which has grown up
around his personality. The most ardent are
not always the most discriminating of readers.
"The fact is," Mr. Ruskin somewhere says,
"that I have always had three different ways of
writing—one, with the single view of making
myself understood, in which I necessarily omit
a great deal of what comes into my head;
another, in which I say what I think ought
to be said; and my third way of writing is
to say all that comes into my head, for my
own pleasure." Amongst the things that
come most freely into Mr. Ruskin's head, and
that give him most pleasure, are somewhat
wilful paradoxes, uttered often, it would seem,
with the single view of making himself mis-
understood. On the other hand, what seldom comes into Mr. Ruskin's head, or what,
if it does come, is generally dismissed as
giving him no pleasure, is the desirability of
saving clauses and qualifying statements. The
consequence is, that nothing is easier for a
captious critic than to convict Mr. Ruskin of
inconsistencies, and for a superficial reader
than to fall into bewilderment. It has seemed

to me, therefore, that I might be doing a real
service, in these days of Ruskin Societies and
Ruskin Reading Guilds, by attempting to set
forth what appeared to me to be the main
and essential drift of his teaching.

To the chapters on Mr. Ruskin's Teaching,
I have added some account of his Work.
Mr. Ruskin, like his master, Carlyle, has
loudly proclaimed himself a Moral Teacher, and
in the case of moral teachers one has a right
to inquire how far they have practised what
they preach. I have not, however, attempted
any estimate of Mr. Ruskin's life and character,
a task for which the time has happily not
arrived. My object has only been to show
such aspects of Mr. Ruskin's public work as
are in themselves of public interest, and incidentally throw light on his teaching. The
best claim, indeed, to honour consists, in Mr.
Ruskin's case, as in that of all great teachers,
not so much in what he has himself done, as
in what he has enabled others to think, and
feel, and do. The highest tribute to Mr. Ruskin's Teaching is to be found in the thoughts
he has inspired and in the characters he has

helped to mould. Nevertheless, many of Mr. Ruskin's own schemes have in themselves a positive value in their generation. They may serve as sign-posts pointing the way to social progress, and they have shown how practical realization may be given to what the late Prince Leopold truly and eloquently described as the last and greatest precept in Mr. Ruskin's Gospel —the precept, namely, "that the highest wisdom and the highest treasure need not be costly or exclusive; that the greatness of a nation must be measured, not alone by its wealth and ap-parent power, but by the degree in which its people have learned together, in the great world of books, of art, and of nature, pure and enno-bling joys."

December 31st, 1889.

In the Second Edition a few phrases have been altered in Part I., and a complete list of Mr. Ruskin's Oxford Lectures has been added; in Part II. some errors of fact have been cor-rected. Otherwise the work is unchanged.

June 30th, 1891.

CONTENTS.

APPENDICES.

NOTES ON MR. RUSKIN'S OXFORD LECTURES.

CONTENTS.

LIST OF ILLUSTRATIONS.

NOTE.

Several chapters in this book originally appeared in the *Pall Mall Gazette*. To the proprietors of that journal I am indebted for kind permission to reprint them here. For the chapter on "The Langdale Linen Industry" I am indebted to my friend Mr. Albert Fleming.

The Illustrations of the Walkley Museum, Meersbrook Park, etc., are from photographs kindly taken for me by Mr. B. Carr and Mr. C. Bradshaw, under the supervision of Mr. William White, the Curator of the Ruskin Museum. For permission to engrave Sir J. E. Boehm's bust of Mr. Ruskin and the Interior of the Ruskin Drawing School—as well as for other kind offices—I am indebted to Mr. A. Macdonald, the Master of the School.

7

PART I.

"THE GOSPEL ACCORDING TO RUSKIN."

CHAPTER I.

PRINCIPLES OF ART.

Is there a Gospel according to Ruskin at all? Is there a "Ruskinian" Gospel? The very genius of Mr. Ruskin as a writer makes the question necessary. Darwin * was no orator as Mr. Ruskin is. There was no glamour of fine writing, no film of ingenious rhetoric, to lend factitious importance or interest to the "Origin of Species." Darwin was the deliverer of a gospel, or he was nothing. But Mr. Ruskin may be a giant of prose writing, and yet have no gospel to deliver. All is not

---

* The preceding article in the series of which this paper formed part was on "The Gospel according to Darwin."

20   A

gold in thought that glisters in words.   It is
with fine words as Mr. Ruskin says of painted
drapery : " As long as they are in their due
service and subjection—while their folds are
formed by the motion of men, and their lustre
adorns the nobleness of men—so long the lustre
and folds are lovely.   But cast them from the
human limbs—golden circlet and silken tissue
are withered; the dead leaves of autumn are
more precious than they."   How, then, is it
with the golden circlets of Mr. Ruskin's periods
and the silken tissues of his phrases ?   He has
shown us a new instrument of expression, but
has he opened any new field of thought or
touched any fresh spring of action ?   Is it
possible to speak of a " Gospel according to
Ruskin " in anything approaching the same
sense as that in which we speak of a " Gospel
according to Darwin " ?   Are there Ruskinians
as well as Darwinians ?   Mr. Ruskin's own
answer to the question, when put in that
form, is a decided negative.   Many men, he
says, have " hope of being remembered as the
discoverers of some important truth, or the
founders of some exclusive system called after
their own names.   But I have never applied

myself to discover anything, being content to praise what had already been discovered; so that no true disciple of mine will ever be a Ruskinian." But now hear some other opinions. " Do you look out," wrote George Eliot to her friend Miss Sarah Hennell, "for Ruskin's books whenever they appear ? . . . I venerate him as one of the great teachers of the age. . . . He teaches with the inspiration of a Hebrew prophet." " Do you read Ruskin's ' Fors Clavigera ' ? " Carlyle asked of Emerson. " If you don't, do, I advise you. Also . . . whatever else he is now writing. There is nothing going on among us as notable to me."

These estimates of Mr. Ruskin himself on the one side, and of his admirers on the other, are not contradictory. The " Gospel according to Ruskin" is one of glad tidings, but not of "news." What George Eliot admired was his teaching of "Truth, Sincerity, and Nobleness." This is an "old, old story." But every age requires the old story to be applied to its new interests and its new temptations. The greatness of Mr. Ruskin depends on the degree in which he has met this twofold need. He took the Gospel of Truth, Sincerity, and Nobleness

An old Gospel with new applications.

as he had learned it from Carlyle, and applied it to a new sphere, untouched by Carlyle and of increasing importance in this time. And secondly, founding his Gospel of Art upon Principles of Life, he re-applied that Gospel in its turn to counteract the besetting materialism and commercialism of his age. In this chapter an attempt will be made to set out, as far as possible in the preacher's own words, the Ruskinian Gospel of Art; whilst in a second chapter some of its leading applications to political and social questions will be considered.

The origin of Art: imitation touched with praise.

It has been said of Carlyle, by one of his latest biographers, that his taste in art was only "that of any Annandale peasant." Then the Annandale peasant must have a great faculty, as indeed the natural man often does have, for going to the root of the matter. "In all true Works of Art," says Carlyle in "Sartor," "if thou know a Work of Art from a Daub of Artifice, wilt thou discern Eternity looking through Time; the Godlike rendered visible." "Art in all times," he says, in "Shooting Niagara," "is a higher synonym for God Almighty's Facts,—which come to us direct from Heaven, but in so abstruse a condition,

and cannot be read at all till the better intellect interpret them. All real Art is definable
as Fact, or say as the disimprisoned Soul of
Fact." In these two passages (the latter of
which, however, was of course long subsequent
to "Modern Painters") is contained the germ
of all Mr. Ruskin's Gospel of Art. What is
Art? From what instinct in man does it spring?
To what faculties does it appeal? By what
rules is it to be judged? What purpose does
it serve? The Ruskinian Gospel answers
these fundamental questions with no uncertain
sound. "The art of man;" such is the first
article of faith as defined in "The Laws of
Fésole," "is the expression of his rational and
disciplined delight in the forms and laws of
the creation of which he forms a part." Mr.
Ruskin's theory of the origin of Art is thus the
old theory of imitation, with a "rider:" Art
arises out of imitation, but of imitation touched
with delight. Both conditions are necessary.
Thus "a lamb at play, rejoicing in its own life
only, is not an artist." But the child who, looking at the lamb and liking it, tries to imitate it
on his slate, is an artist. This is the theory
which all Mr. Ruskin's historical studies in

Art serve to illustrate. "All great Art is Praise." The perfection of the Art of the Greeks⎫ was the expression of their delight in God's⎬ noblest work—the disciplined beauty of the⎭ human body. The perfection of early Italian Art was its delight in "saints a-praising God." It is with architecture as with painting: those fair fronts of mouldering wall were filled with sculpture of the saints whom the cathedral builders worshipped and of the flowers which they loved.

Such being, on the Ruskinian theory, the origin of Art, it is easy to see to what faculties in man it appeals. "Like is known of like:" from delight in the forms and laws of God's creation Art comes; to that delight it appeals. This is the central idea of the chief book of Ruskin's Gospel. "In the main aim and principle of 'Modern Painters,'" he says, "there is no variation from its first syllable to its last. It declares the perfectness and eternal beauty of the work of God, and tests all work of man by concurrence with or subjection to that." Thus, the greatest picture, he says, is that which conveys the greatest number of the greatest ideas. The ideas that can be received from Art are fivefold : ideas of power, ideas of imitation, ideas of truth, ideas of beauty, and ideas of relation (that is, everything productive of expression, sentiment, and character). Of these five sets of ideas, the first two may be classed as one, and soon dismissed—not because they are unimportant, but because the recognition of their importance is included in every Gospel of Art that was ever sanely preached, and besides is felt by every one who ever looked at a picture. "How like it is!" is always the first remark of the unsophisticated critic when he is confronted by a competent picture, and feels a perception of gentle surprice at seeing a piece of canvas covered with pigments looking like a field or a face. The idea of imitation is the first received from a picture; the idea of power—the recognition, that is, of the painter's skill—is perhaps the last.

In this aspect of pictures what artists are so fond of saying—namely, that only artists have the right to criticize them—is true. In one sense it is only the *chef* of the *Café Anglais* who can " do justice " to a dinner at the *Café Riche;* for it is only he who knows how much skill in composition and delicacy in handling

The duty of choosing noble subjects.

are involved in producing the dinner. But no
one has yet pretended that you have no right
to discuss a good dinner unless you could
yourself cook it—and why not ? Because the
dinner itself is to be enjoyed, as well as the
skill which produced it to be admired. And
so it is with pictures : they must be like what
they represent; of course they must; and a
spectator may or may not know how difficult
it is to attain even that, but the more he knows
how difficult is the mastery, the more he will
insist, if he be logical, upon the aim being
worthy. According to Mr. Frith, Turner once
said to Mr. Ruskin, " My dear sir, if you only
knew how difficult it is to paint even a decent
picture, you would not say the severe things
you do of those who fail." As applied to Mr.
Ruskin's criticism of *technique*, the remark may
have been trenchant; as applied to his criticism
of subjects, it cuts precisely the other way.
" The life so short," says Chaucer, " the craft
so long to learne ; " then, for God's sake, do not
waste your hard-won skill and scanty time in
painting a boor instead of a gentleman, or an
" impression " of a ballet-girl instead of a vision
of angel choirs.

And thus we come to the other ideas which "Ideas of Truth." pictures may convey—ideas of truth, of beauty, of relation. Ideas of truth need not detain us. They form a chapter of the Gospel which is indeed supremely important, but also extremely obvious. It was not so when Mr. Ruskin first taught it. The man who in the pre-Ruskinian era was the High Priest among connoisseurs was Sir George Beaumont; and Sir George, admirable man as he was in other respects, when he looked at a landscape, asked, not whether it was true to the facts of nature, but whether it accorded with the fictions of convention. "But where is your brown tree?" he asked of Constable when that painter gave in his adherence to the then revolutionary course of proclaiming that trees were green. No part of Mr. Ruskin's Gospel has won wider acceptance, and in so doing effected a greater revolution in Art, than his vindication of truth in landscape. And one sees whence his success came. "Out of the fulness of the heart the mouth speaketh." To the man who has walked with nature, and seen in it "God Almighty's facts," the conventions of the ideal school are flat blasphemy. "No other man in England," said Carlyle of Mr. Ruskin's political economy, "has in him the same divine rage against falsity." But false wares may be passed in pictures as well as in trade, and Mr. Ruskin's "divine rage" was spent against both alike.

"Ideas of Beauty:" Ruskin at once a Puritan and a Painter.
But it must not be supposed that in preaching Truth in Art he ignores the function of Beauty. On the contrary, it is as an interpreter of Beauty that Mr. Ruskin has probably attracted most readers. The peculiarities of his education have in this respect given him a unique position and insight. He is at once a Puritan and a painter, an Evangelical by training, a Catholic by taste. Hence he has resisted both the Philistinism of Evangelical religion and the frivolity or false sentiment of popular art. To the "æsthetes" in particular he has ever been a deadly enemy, and there is not a line in his books which does not give the lie to the principle, or a rebuke to the practice, of that School. According to it, the essence of Art is beauty, and the essence of beauty consists in its appeal to the senses. This is the theory of the matter which is responsible for all the sensuality and all the frivolity in Art

which made the Puritans banish it as the accursed thing.

Mr. Ruskin's theory of the function of Art is diametrically opposite. According to him, "there is no other definition of the Beautiful, nor of any subject of delight to the æsthetic faculty, than that it is what one noble spirit has created, seen and felt by another of similar or equal nobility. So much as there is in you of ox, or of swine, perceives no beauty and creates none: what is human in you, in exact proportion to the perfectness of its humanity, can create it and receive." Art, he says, is no recreation—it is "not a mere amusement, a minister to morbid sensibilities, a tickler and fanner of the soul's sleep." And this, not because Art is not to give pleasure: on the contrary, it is not Art unless it does; but because the pleasures to which it is the highest function of Art to appeal are the pleasures of the mind, and not of the senses. That such pleasures of the mind are the highest prerogative of man is no new Gospel. It is as old as Aristotle, who defined happiness as "a sort of energy of contemplation." Thus according to Mr. Ruskin, beauty is "the expression

The objective standard of Beauty.

of the creating Spirit of the universe." Neither
is this statement a new one. It was partly
taught by Plato, and more clearly by Spenser,
when he said—

> That Beauty is not, as fond men misdeem,
> An outward show of things, that only seem ;

and when he bade the hearts of men

> Lift themselves up higher
> And learne to love with zealous humble dewty
> Th' eternal fountaine of that heavenly beauty.

It is the detailed proof of this conclusion—oc-
cupying three volumes and a half of " Modern
Painters "—that is the pith of Ruskin's Gospel.
There is, he begins by arguing, an objective
standard of beauty. It is not, as Keats so
prettily but so absurdly said, the true ; for the
" mirage of the desert is fairer than its sands."
Nor is it the useful ; unless the most beautiful
products of art are spades and millstones. Nor
does it depend on custom ; Gower Street may
become less ugly to you if you are used to it,
but it is not custom that is the cause of the
beauty of Giotto's Tower. Nor does it depend
on association of ideas. Associations are a
source of pleasure ; so is beauty ; but beauty is

not therefore association. No; beauty consists, says Ruskin, (1) in certain external qualities of bodies which are *typical* of Divine attributes; (2) in the appearance of felicitous fulfilment of function in *vital* things.

Any reader who wants to get at the evidences of Ruskin's Gospel must study closely the chapters in which the above propositions are worked out. All that can be done here is to take an illustration or two to show the line of argument adopted. Every one has heard of the repose of true beauty; why is repose beautiful? Because it is "a type of Divine permanence," and satisfies

"Typical" and "Vital" Beauty explained.

> The universal instinct of repose,
> The longing for confirmed tranquillity,
> Inward and outward, humble and sublime—
> The life where hope and memory are one.

That is what is meant by *typical beauty*. Again, every one recognizes the beauty of " the ideal ; " but wherein does this beauty consist? Why is the skylark beautiful? Because it so perfectly fulfils the bird-ideal, so happily performs, that is, the highest functions of the songsters of the sky. Why is the face of an ideal man

more beautiful than that of the man in the
street ?   Because Art is "the pure mirror that
can show the seraph standing by each human
body, as signal to the heavenly land."   That is
what is meant by *vital beauty*.   There is no
beauty that cannot ultimately be traced back
to one or other of these causes, and no work
of art which should not be judged by its
compliance with them.   Turner's work is more
beautiful than that of other men, only in the
degree in which it shows more clearly than
they "the disimprisoned soul of fact," and sets
forth more surely "the glory of God."   And
so with architecture.   "The law which it has
been my effort chiefly to illustrate," says Mr.
Ruskin, "is the dependence of all noble design
on the sculpture of organic form."   One school
of architecture sets itself to lines and proportions and conventional ornaments; the other
chooses the suggestion of natural laws, the
imitation of natural forms.   Let the architects
pause, says Mr. Ruskin, with all the seriousness
of a moral teacher, at the parting of "the Two
Paths," before they "wilfully bind up their eyes
from the splendour, wilfully turn their backs
upon all the majesties, of Omnipotence."

One sees from this passage how serious and Art and Religion.
sacred is the mission to which Ruskin's Gospel
summons Art as the interpreter of Beauty.   No
question has been more often debated than
the relation of Art to Religion.   According to
Mr. Ruskin, Art is Religion.   By Religion is
meant " the feelings of love, reverence, or dread
with which the human mind is affected by its
conceptions of spiritual being."   Recognize this
spiritual being, and " name it as you will : " if
you recognize it, and recognizing revere, you
are religious; and Art, as the interpreter of
Beauty, is the prime agent in showing you
noble grounds for such noble emotion.   In
this sense every great artist is necessarily
religious.   The world of Beauty is like the
Beryl in Rossetti's ballad—

" None sees here but the pure alone."

That such has in fact been the case is the
burden of all Mr. Ruskin's books on the history
of artists and art schools.   It is the decadence
of the art of architecture, corresponding with a
decay of vital religion, that he finds written on
the " Stones of Venice ; " the clearness of early
faith that he finds reflected in the brightness of

the pictures of Florence ; the gladness of Greek
religion that gives for him its sharpness to the
"Ploughshare of Pentelicus."

"Ideas of
Relation:"
Art and
Morality.
But in the Gospel according to Ruskin Art
is not only Religion; it is Morality also.   To
understand how this conclusion is reached we
must go back to "ideas of relation," which, it
will be remembered, were the last (and highest)
source of pleasure in Art.   The meaning and
sphere of these ideas can be seen in a moment
by any one who will go into the National
Gallery and look at Turner's "Building of
Carthage," which he bequeathed to the country
to hang side by side with Claude's "Queen of
Sheba."   In the foreground Turner puts a group
of children sailing toy boats.   "The choice of
this incident, as expressive of the ruling passion which was to be the source of future greatness, in preference to the tumult of busy masons
or arming soldiers, has nothing to do with the
technicalities of painting; a scratch of the pen
would have conveyed the same intellectual idea
as an elaborate realization by colour."   Yet this
"idea of relation" gives at once an interest to
the picture which no beauty of forms or colours,
no skill of workmanship, could give.   And not

only that, but it actually enhances the beauty. Take another illustration, and this fact will be seen more clearly. In Turner's "Pass of Faido" the painter introduces a post-chaise in the foreground. He was criticized for so doing, on the ground that he thereby destroyed the majesty of desolation in his picture. Not so; he enhanced it. "The full essence and soul of the scene, and consummation of all the wonderfulness of the torrents and Alps, lay in that post-chaise." And why? Because, without the suggestion of the human element, nature loses in the instant its power over the human heart. Mr. Ruskin has illustrated this point in a famous passage in the "Seven Lamps," descriptive of a scene in the Jura :—

"It would be difficult to conceive one less dependent upon any other interest than that of its own secluded and serious beauty; but the writer well remembers the sudden blankness and chill which were cast upon it when he endeavoured, in order more strictly to arrive at the sources of its impressiveness, to imagine it, for a moment, a scene in some aboriginal forest of the New Continent. The flowers in an instant lost their light, the river its music ; the hills became oppressively desolate ; a heaviness in the boughs of the darkened forest showed how much of their former power had been dependent upon a life which was not theirs, how much

B

of the glory of the imperishable, or continually renewed, creation is reflected from things more precious in their memories than it, in its renewing.   Those ever-spring-ing flowers and ever-flowing streams had been dyed by the deep colours of human endurance, valour, and virtue, and the crests of the sable hills that rose against the evening sky received a deeper worship, because their far shadows fell eastward over the iron wall of Joux and the four-square keep of Granson."

Great Art "the type of strong and noble life."

Herein is another fundamental article in the Gospel according to Ruskin.   It is the function of Art, as we have seen, to declare the beauty of God; but man's soul is the mirror of God's, and hence all the power of nature depends on its subjection to the human soul.   " In these books of mine," says Ruskin, in a central passage of " Modern Painters," " their distinc-tive character as essays on Art is their bring-ing everything to a root in human passion or human hope.   Every principle of painting which I have stated is traced to some vital or spiritual fact ; and in my works on Architecture the preference accorded finally to one school over another is founded on a comparison of their influences on the life of the workman —a question by all other writers on the subject of Architecture wholly forgotten or despised."

The artist, then, and the amateur are not to live in rapt contemplation of a beauty apart from the world of man and the interests of every-day life, but, mixing freely in that world and sharing in those interests, are to show the things that sustain man's spiritual life, and the conditions that minister to his peace. " We live by the sweat of our brow or by the clink of our machinery," says the man of business; "We live not by bread alone, but by admiration, hope, and love," says the artist. Thus it is that "great Art is nothing else than the type of strong and noble life;" for it first "seizes natural facts, and then orders those facts by strength of human intellect, so as to make them, for all who look upon them, to the utmost serviceable, memorable, and beautiful;" and hence, too, it is that so far from Art being immoral, "little else than Art is moral; for if life without industry is guilt, industry without art is brutality."

Such is the Ruskinian Gospel of Art. What is the value of the message to the present generation? To answer that question one has to remember the materialism which, owing to modern science and modern industry, is the

Significance of the foregoing principles to the present age.

besetting danger of the age. The Ruskinian Gospel has sometimes been spoken of as wholly contradictory of both these factors in modern life. If so, it is so much the worse for the Gospel. But in fact, it is not contradictory, but corrective of them. Mr. Ruskin came at the "psychological moment," when science had reduced all life to physical elements, and industry all men to machines, to correct this tendency by showing the other side of truth. Science teaches us that the stars stink, Art that they twinkle; Science that the clouds are "a sleety mist," Art that they are "a golden throne." For Science is of essences, Art of aspects. The one, be it observed, is as much a study of facts as the other. It is as much a fact to be noted in the constitution of things that they produce such and such an effect upon the eye or heart, as that they are made up of certain atoms of matter. And similarly with the conditions of modern industry as with the conclusions of modern science. The drift of modern society under the pressure of economic forces is all towards materialism also—towards the material prosperity of money-getting and the material misery of poverty. The drift of

Mr. Ruskin's teaching is to relieve the pressure of poverty by diverting the race after wealth. The world of industry, with science to do its bidding, placed happiness in wealth. "It got the clouds packed into iron cylinders, and made them carry its wise self at their own cloud pace. It got weavable fibres out of the mosses, and made clothes for itself cheap and fine, and thought that here was happiness." And all the while, as Mr. Ruskin came to preach, "the real happiness of man was placed in the keeping of the little mosses of the wayside and of the clouds of the firmament "—in the keeping of these and in the doing of justice and ministering of mercy. Amid the turmoil of trade and anarchy of competition, Mr. Ruskin proclaimed that "Art still has truth," and bade men "take refuge there." What kind of truth his Gospel teaches in trade and politics, and what kind of refuge it provides, will be shown in the next chapter.

CHAPTER II.

Ruskin's "inquire within upon everything." No gospel is good for anything which is not good for everything. · Confront the novice with some experimental problem upon which your gospel is silent, or with some logical conclusion for which it is not prepared, and what authority is left to you? For you cannot label a gospel like a bale of glass, "This side up only." It must stand four-square to every wind that blows, or it cannot stand at all. It is one of the characteristics of Mr. Ruskin as a writer that he is permeated with a sense of this necessity. "Throughout Ruskin's whole work," says a French critic of to-day, "we find the application of developed theories," and his writings are thus "one of the greatest works achieved by the mind of man." "The teaching of Art," says Mr. Ruskin himself, "is the teaching of all things." And in the fulfilment of this conception

22

of his calling there is no word in his Gospel
of Art which he has not driven home to its
utmost application to life, no interest or sphere
of life which he has not related to some principle of art. He has laid down the law with
equal decision upon Giotto's painting and goose
pies; upon Bible and bicycles; upon railways
and Reynolds; upon the clouds of heaven and
the circles of hell. A complete index to Mr.
Ruskin's works would be a formidable rival to
Mrs. Beeton: you could "inquire within upon
everything."

This enormous multiplicity of topics touched
upon by the preacher makes two general remarks necessary. In the first place, no disciple—even of the straitest sect—is bound to
accept as gospel every word that falls from
the "Master's" lips. A man may be a sincere
and consistent Ruskinian without abjuring to-
bacco or waiting seven years before he marries
his betrothed. For, be it observed, there are
things which appertain to the Gospel, and
things which do not. The Pope is infallible,
but only when he speaks from the chair and
utters the voice of the Church. The judge's
word is law, but only when he delivers the

Distinction
between the
essential
and the
non-essen-
tial in his
Gospel.

judgment of the court, and not when he amuses himself with *obiter dicta*. But on the other hand, this liberty of rejection is strictly limited to such things as are not of the faith. A disciple may not chop a gospel up into morsels, to eat or refuse at his pleasure. This is precisely, however, what most people do with the Gospel according to Ruskin. There has been a curious instance of it in some recent criticisms. In art, says the *Edinburgh*, Mr. Ruskin is often right; in political economy he is always wrong. As a social philosopher, says the *Century*, Mr. Ruskin is above praise; as an art critic, he is beneath contempt. From the point of view of Mr. Ruskin's Gospel both criticisms must necessarily be wrong. For if the teaching of Art be the teaching of everything, "unfaith in aught is want of faith in all."

Ruskin's politics: every man to work out his own salvation.

In order to appreciate the point of contact between Art and life, consider for a moment the only true and vital kind of "historical" art—the art, that is, which represents the living forms and daily deeds of its own time. Teach noble art in this sense, and you become at once a teacher of morality as well.

"Remember," said Mr. Ruskin in one of the
earliest of his public lectures, "that it is not
so much in *buying* pictures as in *being* pictures
that you can encourage a noble school." In
seeking for beauty of form in a marble image,
you necessarily seek also for beauty of character in a living person. "On all the beautiful
features of men and women, throughout the
ages, are written the solemnities and majesty
of the law they knew, with the charity and
meekness of their obedience." The importance
of individual character, the value of work in
forming it, the supremacy of duty in directing
it: these are some of the leading moral lessons
which Mr. Ruskin, like Carlyle, has had to
teach, but to which he has given a new turn
by adding the sanction of Art. It used to be
thought that the "condition of England question" would be solved by the ballot-box, by
fresh liberties, by new laws. Not so, said
Carlyle. Not so, says Mr. Ruskin. In life, as
in Art, the only liberty worth having is founded
on personal discipline. This is why Mr.
Ruskin lays so much stress on the dignity and
usefulness of manual labour. "To succeed to
my own satisfaction," he says, "in a manual

piece of work is life—to me, as to all men."
" Little else except Art," he elsewhere says,
" is wise; all knowledge unaccompanied by a
habit of useful action is too likely to become
deceitful, and every habit of useful action must
resolve itself into some elementary practice of
manual labour." The free hand of the artist
is one (he says) that moves in absolute obedience to felt laws; and the free man is he
who has his passions most perfectly in subjection. And the only way of arriving at this
freedom, in life as in Art, is by apprenticeship
to toil. " To do good work whether we live
or die" is the first article of faith which Mr.
Ruskin demands of his disciples. " Be sure
that you can obey a good law before you seek to
unmake a bad one," was his first injunction to the
" workmen and labourers of Great Britain."

Each man
to be his
brother's
keeper.

That every man must work out his own salvation is the first article of all moral gospels ;
but it requires to be immediately corrected by a
second one, that each man is his brother's keeper.
The growing recognition of this truth is the
leading feature in the social movements of our
generation. By few men has it been enforced
so earnestly as by Mr. Ruskin ; by no one so

eloquently. No one has shown such powerful imagination as he in lifting the veil which hides the grim realities of poverty from the gay dreams of wealth, or such fearless satire in mocking the Churches for "dining with the rich and preaching to the poor." It is only the lack of imagination, Mr. Ruskin argues, that has ever caused the question of Cain to be seriously asked. But if any doubt still lingered, if any sanction on the other side were still needed, the Gospel of Art would supply it. For Art, to be really fine, must, as we have seen, be the representation of beautiful realities, and be pursued in a spirit of delight. And where such conditions are not present, the teacher of Art is necessarily also a social reformer. It is not that he wants to be; he simply cannot help it. There is a passage in "Fors Clavigera," written from Venice, of much interest in this connection :—

How these maxims follow from Ruskin's principles of Art.

"Here is a little grey cockle-shell lying beside me, which I gathered the other evening out of the dust of the island of St. Helena, and a brightly spotted snail-shell, from the thirsty sands of Lido ; and I want to set myself to draw these, and describe them in peace. Yes, and all my friends say that is my business ; why can't I mind it and be happy? . . . But, alas ! my prudent friends, little enough of all that I have a mind to may be permitted me.   For this green tide that eddies by my threshold is full of floating corpses, and I must leave my dinner to bury them, since I cannot save, and put my cockle-shell in cap and take my staff in hand to seek an unencumbered shore."

It would indeed be possible for the artist to build himself a misery-proof studio, as Carlyle built himself a noise-proof study.   But no great work is on such terms possible.   For either the artist must bury himself in idle unrealities —but "it is the vainest of affectations to try to put beauty into shadows, while all real things that cast them are left in deformity and pain,"—or he must be heartless and want-ing in sensibility—but that is to be wanting in just those qualities which distinguish the best art; for fine art is that "in which the hand, the head, and the heart go together." And thus it is that Compassion for the Poor is the last word of Mr. Ruskin's books on Art, as well as of those on Morals.   "I tell you," he said to the Oxford students, as the conclusion of his Art teaching, "that we *may* have splendour of Art again, and with that we may truly praise our Maker, and with that set forth the beauty

and holiness of all that He has made : but only
after we have striven with our whole hearts
first to sanctify the temple of the body and
spirit of every child that has no roof to cover
its head from the cold, and no walls to guard
its soul from corruption, in this our English
land."

But the applications of Mr. Ruskin's Gospel
of Art do not stop with these general counsels
of benevolence. They furnish a system of economics, as well as a standard of morals and
a code of social duty. Mr. Ruskin's Political
Economy—alternately adopted and abused—
follows immediately and vitally from his Art
teaching. The point of connection will come out
most clearly if we consider the National Ideal
which is logically deducible from the orthodox
Political Economy and the tendencies of modern
commerce. This Political Economy taught (or
what is the same thing, was believed to teach*)

Ruskin's
Political
Economy:
his defi-
nition of
wealth.

---

* Herein is to be found, I think, the true justification
of Mr. Ruskin's economic writings. His Political Economy
has been condemned and contemned as based on a complete misunderstanding. He has attacked the science,
it is said, as if it were not a science, but an art. This
is true; but the misconception of the nature and scope of
Political Economy did not begin with Mr. Ruskin. On the

that the road to national prosperity lies in the unchecked and competitive pursuit of material wealth; and the commercial tendencies of the time make England become more and more every day the workshop of the world, until (as Mr. Ruskin puts it) we shall soon arrive at "the state of a squirrel in a cage or a turnspit in a wheel, fed by foreign masters with nuts and dog's meat." Now, it is obvious that a National Ideal such as this is absolutely and entirely

contrary, it began with a certain school of politicians who were eager to interpret the "laws" of Political Economy (*i.e.*, conclusions drawn from abstract assumptions), as if they were laws enforcing political action. As against this perversion of the science, Mr. Ruskin has done great service by insisting (1) "that Political Economy can furnish sound laws of national life and work only when it respects the dignity and moral destiny of man; (2) that the wide use of wealth, in developing a complete human life, is of incomparably greater moment, both to men and nations, than its production or accumulation, and can alone give these any vital significance; (3) that honourable perform-ance of duty is more truly just than rigid enforcement of right; and that not in competition but in helpfulness, not in self-assertion but in reverence, is to be found the power of life." I take this enumeration of Mr. Ruskin's economic principles from the address presented to him at Christmas, 1885, by a large body of his admirers, in-cluding most of the literary and artistic celebrities of the day.

incompatible with any National Art such as
Mr. Ruskin understands. It is incompatible both
in *temper* and in external *conditions.* Hence
Mr. Ruskin was driven to the statement both of
a new *basis* for Political Economy and a new
definition of *wealth.* And just as his theory of
Art led him up to the problem, so also did it
give him the clue to its solution. The greatest
work in Art, he found, had always been done,
not in competition, but in co-operation, not to
sell, but to keep. The application of this idea
to economics is the secret of his system. The
well-being of individuals and nations alike consists, according to him, not in the multitude of
things they possess, but in their virtues and
joys. "The wealth of any country," he laid
down, "is the portion of its possessions which
feeds and educates good men and good women.
The strength and power of a country depend
on the quantity of good men and women in it."

How under existing conditions is the wealth
of England in this sense to be advanced? In
three ways principally. First, by the adoption
in politics of the great principle of " Property to
whom proper "—of land and tools to those who
can use them. Secondly, by planting firmly on

Practical
conse-
quences
therefrom.

English land (including the colonies) as many
men and women as it will support; by the
recognition of "Soldiers of the ploughshare as
well as Soldiers of the Sword;" and generally
by the substitution of the rest of satisfaction
for the unrest of ambition. "The most helpful
and sacred work which can at present be done
for humanity," says Mr. Ruskin, "is to teach
people, not how to better themselves, but how
to satisfy themselves." Follow out these two
ideas of co-operation instead of competition,
of living instead of getting, and you will see
how Mr. Ruskin's economics would release the
pressure upon poverty. So much for the ac-
quisition of wealth. With regard to its distribution he is no equalizer. He teaches not
the wickedness of riches, but their use. Thus,
thirdly and lastly, the National Wealth is to
be promoted by the wise direction of expenditure. Happiness is only to be got out of
honesty, food only out of the ground. These
are two of his leading principles in economics;
but the third is that money is essentially not
a medium of exchange, but a token of right.
And it makes all the difference in the world
whether you use your right to grow "grapes

or grapeshot," and whether when you have got them you use them to preserve life or to destroy. And that being so, just as "that country is the richest which nourishes the greatest number of noble and happy beings," so "that man is richest who, having perfected the functions of his own life to the utmost, has also the widest and most helpful influence, both personal and by means of his possessions, over the lives of others." In such a conception of national economy it is easy to see the large sphere that Art must play—Art that dignifies industry and adorns daily life. "The treasures of true kings," says Mr. Ruskin, in "Sesame and Lilies," "are the streets of their cities ; and the gold they gather, which for others is as the mire of the streets, changes itself for them and their people into a crystalline pavement for evermore."

And now having completed the circle of Ruskin's Gospel, having set out from Art, and having been brought back to it, we are in a position to note in conclusion the relation of the different "sacred books" one to the other. "Modern Painters" taught, on the testimony of the graphic arts, "the claim of all lower nature

The relation of Ruskin's books to each other.

C

on the hearts of men; of the rock, and wave, and herb as a part of their necessary spirit life." The "Stones of Venice" taught, on the testimony of architecture, "the dependence of all human work or edifice, for its beauty, on the happy life of the workman." "Unto this Last" and "Munera Pulveris" taught the laws of that life, and the dependence of National Wealth upon the principles of justice, mercy, and admiration. "Sesame and Lilies" "showed that in a state of society founded on these principles Women will be the guiding and purifying power." In his "Oxford Lectures" Mr. Ruskin preached the necessity that the national life should be led by the upper classes, and "the gracious laws of beauty and labour recognized by them no less than the lower classes of England;" and finally "Fors Clavigera" "showed the relation of these to each other, by declaring first what is visibly salutary—namely, that children should have enough to eat, and their skins be washed clean; and secondly, what is invisibly salutary"—namely, that "in admiration is the chief joy and power of life; admiration for all that is gracious among the living, great among the dead, and marvellous in the Powers that cannot

die." And with all this there is scattered up
and down Mr. Ruskin's books, and finally collected and concentrated in "Fors Clavigera,"
an imperious call to all men who believe the
Gospel to purge their consciences from dead
works and join together in helping their
fellow-men.

In which connection it will not be imper- Ruskin's
tinent to turn for a moment from Mr. Ruskin's preaching and prac-
Gospel to Mr. Ruskin's life, or rather from the tice.
Gospel in words to the Gospel in works; for
Mr. Ruskin is like Chaucer's Parson, who—

> "Christes lore, and His Apostles twelve,
> He taughte, but first he folwede it himselve."

A detailed examination of some aspects of Mr.
Ruskin's works is to be the subject of the
following pages; but here it may be stated
generally that he has spent not a tithe, nor
a half, but the whole of a large fortune in
public and private charities. He has set Miss
Octavia Hill to manage his London property
on principles which have since been adopted
as one of the essentials of latter-day philan-
thropy. He has given his most treasured
drawings and minerals to public galleries and

museums. He has revived village industries
and inspired co-operative undertakings, and he
has established and endowed a Guild which
has for its primary object the redeeming of
waste lands and establishment thereon of well-
ordered lives. Some works are great for what
they accomplish, others for what they suggest.
At present Mr. Ruskin's fame stands on his
achievement as a writer. Twenty years hence
it is conceivable that he may be best remembered for his experiments as a social reformer.
But in Mr. Ruskin's life, as in his Gospel,
the artistic and the social elements cannot be
severed. He is a social reformer because he
is an Art teacher; and whatever is essential
and characteristic in his Art teaching comes
from his social enthusiasm. In Ruskin's Gospel there are diversities of gifts, but it is the
same spirit.

The sanc-
tion of the
Ruskinian
Gospel.

And what, it may be asked, is the sanction,
what the reward of this Gospel ? The sanction
is to be found only in its logical completeness,
the only sure reward in the experience of its
own fulfilment; for as for rewards beyond the
grave, the virtue which Mr. Ruskin has principally taught is that of the Greeks, "whose

notion of heroism was giving one °83, his elec-
kiss, and not getting it." And the eminent-
that he promises to his disciples is b The
"Wild Olive:"—

"The tree that grows carelessly, tufting the rocks
with no vivid bloom, no verdure or branch ; only with
soft snow of blossom, and scarcely fulfilled fruit, mixed
with grey leaf and thorn-set stem ; no fastening of
diadem for you but with such sharp embroidery ! But
this, such as it is, you may win, while yet you live ;
type of grey honour, and sweet rest. Free-heartedness,
and graciousness, and undisturbed trust, and requited
love, and the sight of the peace of others, and the
ministry to their pain ; these, and the blue sky above
you, and the sweet waters and flowers of the earth beneath ; and mysteries and presences, innumerable, of
living things,—may yet be here your riches ; untor-
menting and divine ; serviceable for the life that now
is ; nor, it may be, without promise of that which is to
come."

museums.   F¹
and inspir'
has es⁺
ha⁵

PART II.

SOME ASPECTS OF MR. RUSKIN'S WORK.

CHAPTER I.

MR. RUSKIN AND OXFORD.

A TRENCHANT writer in the *Edinburgh Review*
(October, 1889) has recently called attention to
four different views which may be, and have
been, held of the Professorial Office.   A Professor at Oxford or Cambridge may be appointed for the purpose of Research, or by way
of ornament, or in order to give General Instruction, or lastly with a view to Professional
Teaching.   Mr. Ruskin's tenure of the Slade
Professorship of Fine Art has illustrated each
and all of these different, but not necessarily
conflicting, functions.   In the first instance he
was no doubt elected as the man best able to
combine them all.   When he was reappointed

after an interval of some years, in 1883, his election was due in large measure to the " eminent-man theory " of the professorial office. The inclusion of Mr. Ruskin amongst the Professoriate conferred honour, it was felt, upon the University.* The public, it is curious to note, seems to have thought that such honour as there is in the matter was conferred on Mr. Ruskin, rather than on the University. Even to this day, when he has no longer any claim to the title, he is commonly spoken of and written about as " Professor Ruskin ; " whilst amongst his neighbours and friends he is almost universally known as " the Professor." I am not aware what view Mr. Ruskin himself takes of the distinction thus conferred upon him. Let us hope he values the title more highly than

* " Every one will be delighted to hear that Mr. Ruskin has been re-elected to the Slade Professorship of Art at Oxford. Before it was known that there was any chance of his being willing to resume the office, various excellent suggestions were made for recasting its duties ; but when once Mr. Ruskin consented to stand, there could be only one opinion, which has been expressed by his unanimous election. Genius is not an over-common quality in the occupants of professorial chairs, and any academical body would do itself honour by accepting a man like Mr. Ruskin on his own terms."—*Pall Mall Gazette*, January 17th, 1883.

another famous Oxford Professor, who was "always shy of assuming that honourable style, because," said he, "this is a title I share with so many distinguished men—Professor Pepper, Professor Anderson, Professor Frickle, and others—who adorn it, I feel, much more than I do." *

But Mr. Ruskin's Professorship was very far indeed from being only titular or honorary.   He spent himself freely in carrying out the other functions of a Professor also—the functions of Research, of Education (in the wider sense of that term), and of Professional Teaching.

Under the first of these three heads it is unnecessary to say anything here, for the results of the studies in art history and criticism which Mr. Ruskin undertook in connection with the Slade Professorship are for the most part contained in already published works.   The following is a list of the books which were originally written for his Oxford Lectures † :—

---

* Matthew Arnold (at that time Professor of Poetry at Oxford), in the original Preface to " Essays in Criticism."

† The following is a complete list of Mr. Ruskin's professorial lectures at Oxford.   I am indebted for it to Mr. Sydney C. Cockerell.   The Bibliography referred to is the

"Lectures on Art." (Hilary Term, 1870.)
"Aratra Pentelici." (Michaelmas Term 1870.)

---

elaborate work now being issued to subscribers under the
editorship of Mr. T. J. Wise :—

1870. Hilary Term. "Lectures on Art ;" for dates see Bibliography.
  Michaelmas. "Aratra Pentelici ;" do. do.
1871. 26th Jan. 1st of 3 lectures on "Landscape."
  9th Feb. 2nd do. do.
  23rd Feb. 3rd do. do.
1872. Lent. "Eagle's Nest ;" for dates see Bibliography.
  Michaelmas. "Ariadne Florentina ;" do. do.
1873. 15th and 19th Mar. "Love's Meinie." 1st lecture (Robin).
  2nd and 5th May. Do. 2nd do. (Swallow).
  9th and 12th May. Do. 3rd do. (Chough), not
   yet published.
  Michaelmas. "Val d'Arno" (see Bibliography).
1874. Michaelmas. Course 1. "Mountain Form in the Higher Alps,"
   4 lectures.
   27th Oct. "The Alps and Jura."
   30th Oct. "Alpine Forms produced by Snow."
   3rd Nov. "Alpine Forms produced by Ice."
   6th Nov. "Relations of Æsthetic to Mathematical
   Science of Form."
  Course 2. "Æsthetic and Mathematic Schools of Art in
   Florence," 8 lectures.
   A. Æsthetic Schools of 1300.
    10th Nov. Lecture 1, Arnolfo.
    13th Nov. Lecture 2, Cimabue.
    17th Nov. Lecture 3, Giotto.
   B. Mathematic Schools of 1400
    20th Nov. Lecture 4, Brunelleschi.
    24th Nov. Lecture 5, Quercia.
    27th Nov. Lecture 6, Ghiberti.
   C. Final Efforts of Æsthetic Art in Florence.
    1st Dec. Lecture 7, Angelico.
    4th Dec. Lecture 8, Botticelli.
1875. Michaelmas. "Twelve Lectures on the Discourses of Sir Joshua
  Reynolds," Nov. 2, 4, 6, 9, 11, 13, 16, 18, 20, 23, 25, 27.
1876. No lectures.
1877. Michaelmas. Course of twelve lectures on "Landscape Painting," consisting of twelve readings in "Modern Painters,"

"The Relation between Michael Angelo and Tintoret." *

"The Eagle's Nest." (Lent Term, 1872.)

"Ariadne Florentina." (Michaelmas Term, 1872.)

"Love's Meinie." (Lent and Easter Terms, 1873.)

"Val d'Arno." (Michaelmas Term, 1873.)

"The Art of England." (Lent, Easter, and Michaelmas Terms, 1883.)

"The Pleasures of England." (Michaelmas Term, 1884.)

Besides these lectures delivered at Oxford, Mr. Ruskin undertook in connection with his Professorship a series of Foreign Guide-books. "It seems to me," he said ("Mornings in Florence," p. 1), "that the real duty involved in my Oxford Professorship cannot be completely done by giving lectures in Oxford only, but that I ought also to give what guidance I may to travellers in Italy." The books issued in execution of this self-imposed duty are—

---

collating the passages which the author thinks likely to be permanently useful (see Appendix I.).

1883. Michaelmas. "Art of England" (see Bibliography).

1884. Michaelmas. "Pleasures of England" &c. (see Bibliography and Appendices II.-V.).

* This lecture, published separately in pamphlet form, for the convenience of travellers, was the last of the preceding course.

"Mornings in Florence." Six chapters of "Simple
  Studies of Christian Art for English Travellers."
"St. Mark's Rest." An essay in "The History of
  Venice, Written for the Help of the Few Tra-
  vellers who still Care for her Monuments."
"Guide to the Principal Pictures in the Academy
  of Fine Arts at Venice. Arranged for English
  Travellers."

To which should perhaps be added the "Separate Travellers' Edition" of Chapter iv. of the
"Bible of Amiens," being a guide-book to Amiens
Cathedral. This is not the place for entering
upon any critical estimate of Mr. Ruskin's later
writings upon Art, but the foregoing lists will
show that in point of quantity Mr. Ruskin has
a creditable record of Research to show for
the ten years of broken health during which
he held his Oxford Professorship.

But it is not only, or chiefly, in virtue of his
professorial writings that Mr. Ruskin's connection with Oxford has left an enduring monument behind it. The writer in the *Edinburgh
Review* above quoted condemns the educational theory of professorships, no less than
the "eminent-man theory," as an obsolete sur-
vival from mediæval days; and Carlyle said
that "the true University of these days is a

Collection of Books" ("Heroes," Lecture V.). There is a large element of truth in this point of view: larger, perhaps, than the Universities have as yet recognized. But however wide may be the dispersion of books, there will always remain a place in the educational system for the Living Teacher and the Living Voice. Mr. Ruskin's Professorship at Oxford was notable for the full use he made of these two opportunities. No Professor, I suppose, has had more power of personal influence over his pupils, or has used it more for good, than Mr. Ruskin.* One of the methods which he

* Amongst other well-known men who were much under Mr. Ruskin's influence at Oxford were Mr. W. H. Mallock and the late Prince Leopold. Mr. Ruskin somewhere refers to Mr. Mallock's "Is Life Worth Living?" as "faultlessly logical;" and Mr. Mallock described Mr. Ruskin, in "The New Republic," under the disguise of "Mr. Herbert" —the only portrait in that clever book which is not also a caricature. "He is almost the only man of these days," some one is made to say of "Mr. Herbert," "for whom I feel a real reverence—almost the only one of our teachers who seems to me to speak with the least breath of inspiration." Prince Leopold also entertained a warm admiration for and friendship with Mr. Ruskin, to whose work the Prince, in his first public address, paid the following high tribute:—

"It is not only at Cambridge that it will be felt that men of culture and of learning hardly have a worthier aim than

adopted for gathering a circle of ardent young men around him, and impregnating them with his spirit, was the subject of much sarcastic comment. This was the famous road-digging experiment. No one was more alive to the amusing side of the affair than Mr. Ruskin himself. The road which his pupils made is, he has been heard to admit, about the worst

to carry their higher thoughts and more cultivated know-ledge into many homes which perhaps have no other ways of making progress. Of such aims we, at Oxford, have a great and striking example. We have seen a man in whom the highest gifts of refinement and of genius reside, who yet has not grudged to give his best to others; who has made it his main effort—by gifts, by teaching, by sympathies —to spread among the artisans of villages and the labourers of our English fields the power of drawing a full measure of instruction and happiness from this wonderful world, which rich and poor alike gain from. We have seen such a man in Professor Ruskin; and among all the lessons which those who have had the privilege of his teaching and his friendship must have carried with them for life, none, I think, can have sunk deeper than the last: that the highest wisdom and the highest treasure need not be costly or exclusive; that the greatness of a nation must be measured, not alone by its wealth and apparent power, but by the degree in which its people have learned together, in the great world of books, of art, and of nature, pure and ennobling joys." (Speech at the Mansion House, in sup-port of the London Society for the Extension of University Teaching, February 19th, 1879.)

in the three kingdoms, and for any level places
in it he gives the credit to his gardener, whom
he incontinently summoned from Brantwood.
Nevertheless the experiment, even from the
point of view of road-making, was by no means
barren. An inch of practice is worth a yard
of preaching; and Mr. Ruskin's road-digging
at Hincksey gave a powerful stimulus to the
Gospel of Labour,* of the same kind as the
later and independent stimulus of Count Tolstoi,
of whom Mr. Ruskin has spoken gratefully in
recent years as his successor. But the fact
is, that most of the Oxford road-diggers were
attracted to the work, not for its own sake, but
for the reward of it—the reward of the subsequent breakfast-party and informal talks in
Mr. Ruskin's rooms at Corpus. It was in Mr.
Ruskin's Oxford Lectures .and these supplementary enforcements of their teaching that the
seeds were sown, or watered, of that practical
interest in social questions which is the "Oxford movement" of to-day. Among the under-
graduate road-diggers was Arnold Toynbee,
who rose by his zeal to the rank of foreman.

* See, for instance, an article on "The New School," in
the *Pall Mall Gazette*, August 26th, 1889.

"He was thus entitled," adds his biographer, "to appear frequently at those breakfasts which Mr. Ruskin gave to his young friends, and enlivened with quaint, eloquent conversation. Upon men like Toynbee intercourse with Mr. Ruskin had a stimulating effect more durable than the actual improvement of the road near Hincksey. Toynbee came to think very differently from Mr. Ruskin upon many subjects, and especially upon democracy, but always regarded him with reverence and affection."* It is impossible to say in how many leaders and followers of the "young Oxford" movement Mr. Ruskin's influence worked directly or indirectly as a stimulus and an inspiration. What is certain is, that the actual course taken by that movement has followed the principles preached by Mr. Ruskin. "I tell you," said the Professor of Fine Art, at the close of one of his lectures, "that neither sound art, policy, nor religion can exist in England until, neglecting, if it must be, your own pleasure-gardens and pleasure-chambers, you resolve that the streets which are the habitation of the poor, and the

---

* "Arnold Toynbee." By F. C. Montague. (Baltimore; Johns Hopkins University.)

fields which are the playgrounds of their children, shall be again restored to the rule of the
spirits, whosoever they are, in earth and heaven,
that ordain and reward, with constant and conscious felicity, all that is decent and orderly,
beautiful and pure." It is the conviction of
this truth that has led to the Universities'
Settlements in East London. "My University
friends came to me," says Mr. Ruskin, "at the
end of my Inaugural Lectures, with grave faces,
to remonstrate against irrelevant and Utopian
topics being introduced." * Now that the
Utopia is beginning to be realized, the rele-
vance of it is more apparent. Sermons, like
trees, must be judged by their fruits.

Mr. Ruskin's first professorial lecture at
Oxford, it may be interesting to say, was announced for the theatre in the Museum, but so
great was the crowd that the Professor and
his audience adjourned to the large Sheldonian

---

* Mr. Mallock has "taken off" such remonstrances very
cleverly in "The New Republic." "What a dreadful
blowing-up Mr. Herbert gave us!" he makes one of the
characters say. "Now that, you know, I think is all very
well in a sermon, but in a lecture, when the things are
supposed to be taken more or less literally, I think it is a
little out of place."

Theatre. This, however, was an exception, and the usual lecture-room was in the Museum.* The crowd was always very great, and it was necessary to be outside the doors an hour beforehand to secure a good seat. At the first lecture of his second Professorship there was a large sprinkling of ladies; subsequently tickets were issued, which were confined (with a few exceptions) to members of the University. On many occasions Mr. Ruskin repeated his lectures twice in the week, in order to give every one who wished to hear him a chance. The attendance of undergraduates was invariably very large. This was the more remarkable as the lectures were always given in the afternoon, which is ordinarily at Oxford devoted to other purposes than the pursuit of learning. Mr. Ruskin's lectures were further remarkable for the number, comparatively large, of graduates which they attracted. At the first lecture of his second Professorship the then Vice-Chancellor (Professor Jowett) attended

---

* This is the "Oxford Museum," in the formation and building of which Mr. Ruskin took so lively an interest. See "Arrows of the Chace," i. 1812–13, and "The Oxford Museum" (1860).

in state with the proctors, and rose at the end to say a few graceful words of welcome and thanks, which were received with a storm of applause.

But the charm of the Living Voice in Mr. Ruskin's lectures was as potent as the influence of the Living Teacher. The published volumes of these lectures are amongst the more important, as they are the most closely and carefully written, of his works. But they convey to the reader only a faint echo of the fascination they exercised over the hearer.*

Mr. Ruskin, is, indeed, no orator. His eloquence is studied, not spontaneous—the eloquence of a writer, not of a speaker. His voice, though sympathetic, is neither strong nor penetrating. Of action he has little or none. But one quality which is essential to a successful speaker Mr. Ruskin possesses to the full—the

---

* "I have heard him lecture several times at the Royal Institution," says Mr. Mallock, in "The New Republic," "and that singular voice of his, which would often hold all the theatre breathless, haunts me still, sometimes. There was something strange and aërial in its exquisite modulations, that seemed as if it came from a disconsolate spirit, hovering over the waters of Babylon and remembering Sion."

quality of a striking personality. No one who ever attended his Oxford Lectures is likely to forget the bent figure with the ample gown—discarded often when its folds became too hopelessly involved—and the velvet college cap, one of the few remaining memorials of the "gentleman commoner." Mr. Ruskin is a great believer in the importance of distinctive dress.* The habit with him does, or should, show the man. And certainly in his own case the quaintness of his costume—the light home-spun tweed, the double-breasted waistcoat, the ill-fitting and old-fashioned frock-coat, the amplitude of inevitable blue tie †—accurately reflected something of the quaintness of his mind and talk. If it were not for the peculiarly delicate hands and tapering

---

* See, for instance, "Eagle's Nest," p. 212; "Two Paths," p. 111; "Fors," 1872, xv. p. 9; and "Val d'Arno," p. 82, in which latter passage Mr. Ruskin argues, with an element of truth, that the history of the world might have been different if soldiers had always been dressed in black instead of in red, and monks in red instead of in black. . I have heard amusing stories told of the too literal adoption of "the Master's" views on costume by some of his disciples.

† The following is an item from "Affairs of the Master," as given in "Fors" (1876, p. 297):—

"July 16. Geoghegan (blue neckties) . . . £4 0 0."

fingers, denoting the artistic temperament, the
Oxford Professor might have been taken for
an old-fashioned country gentleman. In repose
Mr. Ruskin's face has of recent years been fur-
rowed into sadness; but the blue eyes,* pierc-
ing from beneath thick, bushy eyebrows, have
never ceased to shine with the fire of genius;
whilst the smile that was never long absent
when he lectured, lit up his face with the radi-
ance of a singularly gracious and gentle spirit.

Mr. Ruskin has sometimes been accused of
lack of humour—an accusation made of most
men who are in earnest. That the Professor
of Fine Art took both himself and his subjects
seriously was very obvious; but not less obvious to any one who ever heard him lecture
was his saving sense of humour. Just as an
ever-recurring smile relieved an expression of
prevailing sadness, so a play of humour relieved
the sternness of teaching. "As solid as the
lecture of a University Professor" was a comparison recently applied to the discourse of

---

* Speaking of portraits of him, Mr. Ruskin says, in
"Præterita" (ii. 73), "I will be thus far proud as to tell the
disappointed spectator, once for all, that the main good of
my face, as of my life, is in the eyes—and only in those
seen near."

some politician. Mr. Ruskin's earlier Oxford
Lectures had much solid stuff in them, but no
lecturer knew better than he how to relieve
the strain by supplying those *diverticula amœna*
—those pleasant digressions—which are the
salt of oral discourse. Mr. Ruskin's fads and
fancies have often been laughed at, but by no
one more heartily than by himself. It was the
frequent digressions in the form of self-depre-
catory egoism that gave a peculiar charm to
Mr. Ruskin's Lectures, by investing them with
what the French call *intimité*, with the personal note of familiar conversation. A lecture
delivered some years ago, at the London Institution (December 4th, 1882), afforded at the
very outset a case in point. The subject originally announced was " Crystallography," but it
had subsequently been changed to " Cistercian
Architecture," and one of the newspapers had
remarked that " no doubt either title would do
equally well." Mr. Ruskin began by referring
to this remark, and admitted that there was a
good deal of truth in ít, for " in the proposed
lecture on Crystallography there would certainly
have been allusions to Cistercian Architecture,
while it had required all his powers of self-

denial to keep Crystallography out of the lecture
he was actually delivering.   He was not equally
successful in including Cistercian Architecture,
and he was amused to find that his lecture was
five-parts written before any allusion to the
architecture in question came in.   However,
stones had always been interesting to him only
as expressing the minds of their builders ; and
the main part of the lecture was occupied with a
delightful sketch of the principles and methods
of the Benedictine monks, with their gospel of
manual labour, and their good work in agri-
culture and letters.   Then followed an equally
charming description (illustrated by diagrams)
of the Monastery of Cluny, which was con-
trasted, in Mr. Ruskin's manner, with a picture
of our modern rural economy—with a parson
looking on at the 'restoration' of his church,
while the squire was busy with plans for
agricultural machinery, which would send the
people off to America." *   At Oxford, where he
spoke " among friends, with the chaff of the
citizens winnowed out," Mr. Ruskin permitted

* *Pall Mall Gazette*, December 5th, 1882. A fuller
report of the lecture, with plan, appeared in the *Art
Journal* for 1883, pp. 46-9.

himself greater license in colloquial banter.
He was often behindhand with the preparation
of his lectures, and sometimes he could not
even get through the regulation hour by Charles
Lamb's expedient of making up for beginning
late by ending early.   I remember one occasion, during the course on "The Pleasures of
England," when he found some difficulty in
eking out the time, even with the help of copious extracts from himself and Carlyle; but
he kept his audience in good humour by con-
fessing to some "bad shots" in previous lectures; by telling them that all pretty girls were
angels; by abusing "the beastly hooter" that
woke them every morning, and assuring them
that, in spite of appearances, he really was not
humbugging them.   The digressions and in-
terpolations in Mr. Ruskin's Oxford Lectures
were, however, by no means confined to pretty
fooling; often they were passages of serious
and telling eloquence.   I remember one such in
the lecture on "The Pleasures of Faith" (see
p. 223), when he turned aside from his manuscript notes to refer to General Gordon as a
Latter-day Saint whose life still illustrates the
age of faith.   We are too much in the habit,

Mr. Ruskin had been saying, of "supposing that temporal success is owing either to worldly chance or to worldly prudence, and is never granted in any visible relation to states of religious temper"—as if the whole story of the world, read in the light of Christian faith, did not show "a vividly real yet miraculous tenour" in the contrary direction! "But what need," Mr. Ruskin broke off to say, "to go back to the story of the world when you can see the same evidence in the history of to-day—in the lives and characters of men like Havelock and Gordon?" Often, too, the lecturer would lay aside his manuscript at some important point, and giving free play to his feelings, drive it home in burning passages of extempore irony. Hence the published lectures, printed from his manuscript, often differed greatly from the lectures as actually delivered; and therefore I have thought it might be interesting to give, in an Appendix, besides some notes of unpublished lectures, my abstracts, made at the time, of a few published ones.

Another thing which gave special interest to the Spoken Lecture, as distinct from the Printed

Word, does not, unhappily, admit of similar sampling. This is the copious illustration of the lectures' by means of drawings, diagrams, and pictures, upon which Mr. Ruskin used at Oxford to spend incredible pains. Those who have heard his lectures in London will be already familiar with this characteristic. At the Royal Institution, for instance, when lecturing on Flamboyant Architecture, Mr. Ruskin prepared quite a considerable exhibition of pictures, drawings, and photographs.* On a more recent occasion, too, at the London Institution, it will be remembered how the lectures on "The Storm-cloud of the Nineteenth Century" were illustrated by a series of coloured pictures executed by Mr. Arthur Severn from drawings by Mr. Ruskin ("kept bottled like his father's sherries"), and thrown on a screen by means of Mr. Wilson Barrett's limelight. But at Oxford, where Mr. Ruskin had the double purpose of illustrating his lectures and enriching the University collec-

* A catalogue of "References to the Series of Paintings and Sketches, from Mr. Ruskin's Collection, shown in Illus-. tration of the Relations of Flamboyant Architecture to Contemporary and Subsequent Art, at the Evening Meeting of the Royal Institution, Friday, January 29th, 1869," is one of the rarer Ruskin pamphlets.

tions, his system of illustration was yet more lavish and elaborate. The specimens which he was in the habit of exhibiting in his lectures may be divided into two classes—(1) standard and permanent works of art, and (2) diagrams, copies, and enlargements prepared specially to illustrate or enforce some passing point. Many specimens of the former sort, and a few of the latter, may still be seen in the cabinets of the " Ruskin Drawing School" (see next chapter). For purposes of illustration in this sort Mr. Ruskin had the University galleries as well as his own collections to draw upon, and any student who attended all the Slade Professor's lectures had the advantage of examining at one time or another a large and unique gallery of art under the immediate guidance of the great critic. The large table in the theatre and the wall behind were generally covered with drawings and pictures ; most of these would be referred to in the course of the lecture, whilst at the end there would be a rush to the front, and the Professor would hold an informal " class " (as the University Extensionists call it) for further explanation and criticism of the pictures to such students as cared to stay. But it was the ingenuity expended in the preparation of temporary illustrations that gave unique interest to Mr. Ruskin's Oxford Lectures. The few illustrated volumes of these lectures that have been published will give the reader some idea of the care which the Professor bestowed on this portion of his teaching. But only a few of the diagrams and pictures exhibited at the lecture-room have ever been reproduced in book form. Mr. Macdonald, the talented and zealous master of the Ruskin Drawing School, must have a large collection of them, for it was upon his willing hands that the work of preparing the Professor's whimsical illustrations mostly fell. References to some of these will be found in the reports of the lectures on "The Pleasures of England" which are given in the Appendix. Many more were exhibited during the preceding course on "The Art of England." The Fifth Lecture, for instance—that on "John Leech and John Tenniel"—was illustrated by the original drawing for the frontispiece of *Punch*, and by several enlarged reproductions of Mr. Du Maurier's drawings—some photographed by Miss Kate Greenaway's brother, and others "drawn more faithfully than any photographer could do, by Mr. Macdonald." There was always a large element of the unexpected in Mr. Ruskin's illustrations (as there is in his writings). Generally amongst the pictures placed beforehand on the wall behind the lecturer, there would be one with its face turned to the wall, or two or three would be brought in at the last moment, carefully covered up, by Mr. Ruskin's servant. The audience would always smile in anticipation on such occasions, for they knew that some pretty jest or curious fancy was in store. Great was the amusement on one occasion when a hidden treasure was disclosed in the shape of a sketch from Tintoret's "Paradise," which the Professor—by chance or design—held out wrong side up. "Ah, well," he said, joining in the general laughter, "what does it matter? for in Tintoret's 'Paradise' you have heaven all round you." In the last lecture of "The Art of England" also there was a characteristic incident. Mr. Ruskin was contrasting the way in which modern French art looks at the sky with that in which Turner saw and drew "the pure traceries of the vault of morning." "See," he said, "what the French artistic imagination makes of it," and a drawing

done by Mr. Macdonald from a French handbook was disclosed, showing the clouds grouped
into the face of a mocking and angry fiend.
When the audience had had their look and
their laugh, Mr. Macdonald modestly proceeded
to turn his sketch with its back to the wall
again. "No, no!" interposed Mr. Ruskin,
"keep it there, and it shall permanently remain in your school, as a type of the loath-
some and lying spirit of defamation which
studies man only in the skeleton and nature
only in ashes."

But perhaps the most effective piece of what
may be called the lecturer's stage-play was one
which occurred in the "Readings in 'Modern
Painters'" (see Appendix I.). Mr. Ruskin was
expatiating, as was his wont, on the vandalism
of the modern world. On an easel beside
him was a water-colour drawing by Turner of
Leicester. "The old stone bridge is picturesque," he said, "isn't it? But of course you
want something more 'imposing' now-a-days.
So you shall have it." And taking his paint-box
and brush, Mr. Ruskin rapidly sketched in on
the glass what is known in modern specifications
as a "handsome iron structure." "Then," he

continued, "you will want, of course, some tall factory chimneys, and I will give them to you galore." Which he proceeded to, in like fashion. "The blue sky of heaven was pretty, but you cannot have everything, you know." And Mr. Ruskin painted clouds of black smoke over the Turner sky. "Your 'improvements,'" he went on, "are marvellous 'triumphs of modern industry,' I know; but somehow they do not seem to produce nobler men and women, and no modern town is complete, you will admit, without a gaol and a lunatic asylum to crown it. So here they are for you." By which time not an inch of the Turner drawing was left visible under the "improvements" painted upon the glass. "But for my part," said Mr. Ruskin, taking his sponge, and with one pass of the hand wiping away those modern improvements against which he has inveighed in vain in so many printed volumes—"for my part, I prefer the old."

CHAPTER II.

IN the previous chapter some account has been
given of Mr. Ruskin's Oxford Professorship
so far as his lectures and general educational
influence were concerned. It remains to say
something of his Professional Teaching in the
criticism and practice of Art. Mr. Ruskin, it
should be remembered, had in this matter to
create his own duties. The Professorship of
Fine Art was founded in 1869, in pursuance of
the will of Mr. Slade, and Mr. Ruskin was the
first Professor elected. It fell to him, therefore, to organize a new study in the University
on his own lines. The conception which he
formed of his duties was clearly defined in his
Inaugural Lectures, and in the less accessible
catalogues referred to therein. "A youth is
sent to the Universities," he said, "not to be
apprenticed to a trade, nor even always to be

advanced in a profession, but always to be
made a gentleman and a scholar." He con-
ceived it, therefore, to be "the function of this
Professorship to establish both a practical and
critical School of Fine Art for English gentlemen : practical, so that if they draw at all, they
may draw rightly; and critical, so that they
may both be directed to such works of existing
art as will best reward their study, and enabled to make the exercise of their patronage
of living artists delightful to themselves by their
consciousness of its justice, and to the utmost
beneficial to their country, by being given only
to the men who deserve it." It was in order to
carry out this double function of the Slade Professorship that the "Ruskin Drawing School"
was established. The school has two sides:
first, it includes a large, unique, and very valuable collection of works of art; secondly, it is
a School of Art, under a master appointed by
Mr. Ruskin. The formation of the collections
was necessary in order—as Mr. Ruskin explained to his pupils—"to call your attention,
by precision of copying, to the qualities of good
art, and to give you, yourselves, such power of
delineation as may assist your memory of visible

things, and enable you to explain them intelligibly to others." The establishment of a School of Art under a special master was necessary in order to carry out Mr. Ruskin's special theories of Art education. "After carefully considering," he wrote in 1871, "the operation of the Kensington system of Art-teaching throughout the country, and watching for two years its effects on various classes of students at Oxford, I became finally convinced that it fell short of its objects in more than one vital particular; and I have, therefore, obtained permission to found a separate Mastership of Drawing in connection with the Art Professorship at Oxford; and elementary schools will be opened in the University galleries, next October, in which the methods of teaching will be calculated to meet requirements which have not been contemplated in the Kensington system" ("Fors Clavigera," 1871, ix. p. 19). These two sides of the Drawing School—the School of Art and the collection of specimens—were developed by Mr. Ruskin with characteristic zeal and generosity. He began to accumulate his specimens immediately on his appointment to the Professorship, and he added to them throughout his

E

tenure of it.   In 1872 the University assigned
the western wing of its galleries in Beaumont
Street to the purpose of the Ruskin Drawing
School, and Mr. Ruskin on his side gave to the
University a sum of £5000 for the school's
endowment.   The Master of Drawing appointed
by Mr. Ruskin was Mr. Alexander Macdonald,
to whose steady teaching the Professor bore
repeated testimony, and who, happily, still occupies the post.

As a School of Art for University students
the Ruskin Drawing School has not been a success.   Its founder did not, indeed, begin with
any great expectations.   He was more anxious,
as every University Professor should be, to lay
down standard principles of teaching than to
attract large numbers of scholars.   " It matters
comparatively little," he said, " whether few or
many of our students learn to draw; but it matters much that all who learn should be taught
with accuracy" ("Aratra Pentelici," p. viii.).
But those who learned were, I fear, fewer than
Mr. Ruskin hoped even in his least sanguine
moments.   " As for the undergraduates," he said
in 1883, "I never succeeded in getting more than
two or three of them into my school, even in its

palmiest days." *   In the preface to the new
edition of his Inaugural Oxford Lectures (1887),
Mr Ruskin ascribes the failure to faults, or
circumstances, in him.   " It would have been
necessary to my success," he says, "that I
should have accepted permanent residence in
Oxford, and scattered none of my energy in
other tasks.   But I chose to spend half my
time at Coniston Waterhead, and to use half
my force in attempts to form a new social
organization—the St. George's Guild—which
made all my Oxford colleagues distrustful of
me, and many of my Oxford hearers contemptuous."   He does not, he added at the same
time, retract one word of hope for the success
of other masters.   I have not heard, however,
that the other Slade Professors have made any
more progress than did Mr. Ruskin in estab-
lishing a practical School of Art amongst the
Oxford students.   Unless and until Fine Art is
added to the University curriculum, and to the
schools in which degrees may be obtained, any
such hope is chimerical.   Moreover, the atmos-

---

* On a recent visit to the Drawing School I found these
palmy days continuing.   In the morning there was a full
class of ladies.   In the afternoon, set apart for undergraduates, the number of students was two.

phere of the Universities does not seem con-
ducive to excellence in the arts. How very
few of our artists have come, either in the past
or in the present, from the Universities! * But
though the undergraduates held back, the young
ladies of Oxford came forward, and from the
institution of the school until now it has been
largely and regularly attended by them. The
system of teaching carried out by Mr. Macdonald, under Mr. Ruskin's instructions, is that
defined in the Inaugural Lectures (see especially Lecture V.). Its distinctive feature, it
will be remembered, is that, whereas students
generally learn to draw details first, and to
colour and mass them afterwards, in the Ruskin
Drawing School they learn to arrange broad
masses and colours first, and to put in details
afterwards. With regard to the order in which
different objects are studied, the following "Note
by Professor Ruskin" was issued on his re-
sumption of the Slade Professorship in 1883 :—

"I leave for the present to Mr. Macdonald's experience and judgment the direction of the junior students
in the Ruskin schools, and have arranged the following

---

* Amongst eminent living artists I can think of none who
was educated at the University besides Mr. Briton Rivière
and Mr. Burne-Jones.

scheme of work for students of either sex entering our
classes from the age of sixteen and upwards, adapting
the exercises enforced especially to the conditions of
University life, but yet arranging them with the collateral view of their probable introduction in schools where
more consistent attention to the subject of Art could
be given than is possible in connection with the courses
of reading at present necessary to distinction in Oxford.
The pass certificates, however, will ultimately be given
only to students who have attained such a degree of
skill as must imply their having attended in the school
with steadiness during the whole period of their residence in the University, giving at least a couple of hours
in each week out of their best and untired time, and
supplementing the work done in residence by some
consistent practice during vacations.

"In the first year the student will be required to ·
attain steadiness and accuracy in the outline of simple
forms, and ease in the ordinary processes of pure water-
colour painting; that is to say, he must learn to lay
smooth tints within spaces of complex shape without
transgressing their limits, and over spaces of large
extent with equality and smoothness.   The actual
exercises given will be primarily map-drawing, with
the necessary projections of the sphere, and such
colouring and shading as may sufficiently express the
character of the country ; next, the delineation of *the
primary types of good architectural construction;* and,
in association with these, exercise in the elements of
ornamental design in colour and form ; the drawings
being carried forward to approximate completion in
light and shade.

"The second year will be given to the study of
landscape, completing in connection with it that of

architecture, so as to form the student's taste and judgment in that art, and to increase to the utmost degree
possible his enjoyment of the historic buildings, the
natural phenomena, and the organic beauty of the
inanimate world.

"In the third year he will be required to draw from
the beautiful forms of life, distinguishing the characters
in which such beauty consists from those of awkward-
ness or deformity, and to copy a certain number of
examples of figure-painting, such as may sufficiently
direct, and in part form, his taste in the highest walks
of art, while he is assisted and encouraged at the same
time in the rapid sketching, both of animals and figures,
from nature, so as to give him interest in familiar
scenes and daily incidents."

This note proved, however, somewhat of a
brutum fulmen. The Professor had given orders
—so he explained in the course of the first
lecture on "The Pleasures of England"—that
no pupils should be admitted who were not
prepared to conform to his edict; but this
"modest ordinance" having had the effect of
emptying the school of its former pupils, and
not having tempted new scholars, it was subsequently withdrawn, and the young ladies of
Oxford were once more to be admitted "to copy
Turner in their own way." Whether owing to
this licence or to other causes, the Drawing
School is now well attended by them. Probably

if the exceptional advantages of it were better known, it would be better attended still. In Mr. Macdonald the school has a most capable and conscientious master. In Mr. Ruskin's collections, which will presently be described, there is a series of educational examples un-rivalled by any other in the country. The adjoining University galleries are rich in old masters, in antique sculptures, and in vases and other similar objects. They contain, moreover, partly by gift from Mr. Ruskin, partly on loan from the National Gallery, a superb set of Turner drawings; while the collection of drawings in pen and chalk by Michael Angelo and Raphael is one of the finest in Europe. There is, further-more, in the galleries an adequate Fine Art Library; whilst the eminently practical lectures and demonstrations given by the present Slade Professor, Mr. Herkomer, R.A., afford oppor-tunities for instruction which few (if any) schools of art offer on similarly easy terms. On its practical side the Ruskin Drawing School de-serves far greater success than it commands.

The same remark applies with equal force to the collections contained in the school. These collections have all been catalogued by Mr.

Ruskin, who has added explanatory or descriptive notes to many of the items, and referred at length to several others, in his writings.   But the catalogues are so scarce and little known that some general account of the collections, based on a personal examination, may be of interest to students of Mr. Ruskin.   Of the pictures and drawings placed on the walls of his school, Mr. Ruskin gives the following account :

"In the alcove I have placed one of my own studies from a fresco of Luini's at Milan ;* with two original designs by Edward Burne-Jones, 'Love Bringing Back Alcestis from the Grave,' and 'The Two Wives of Jason.' These two drawings and the original of my study are consummate in dignity and purity of conception, and the best examples I can give of the forms of highest art which I think should be held, for standard and scope, by English students.

"On the west side of this portion of the room is Tintoret's sketch for his picture of the Doge Avice

---

* Speaking of the colour of gules—a full soft scarlet, not dazzling, but warm and glowing—Mr. Ruskin says, "It is used, in opposition to darker purple, in large masses, in the fresco painting of later Rome ; is the dominant colour of ornamental writing in the Middle Ages (giving us the ecclesiastical term *rubric*), and asserts itself finally, and most nobly, in the fresco paintings of Ghirlandajo and Luini. I have tried to represent very closely the tint of it Luini has given to St. Catherine's mantle, in my study in your schools" ("Eagle's Nest," § 226).

Mocenigo praying. This sketch, once belonging to Baron Rumohr, is full of interest and of exemplary qualities. The other paintings or drawings on the walls have been made under my direction for the illustration of architecture ; except the Copley Fielding at the end of the room, which is an instructive example of water-colour painting of the old school, executed by washed tints ; and my own study from the Castel-barco tomb at Verona, on the right-hand side of the door, in going out, which is left in its unfinished state to show the mode of striking colour at once frankly on the white paper which I wish the students more generally to adopt.

"None of these paintings or drawings are, as yet, formally presented to, or accepted by, the University. Some do not deserve any permanent position ; and I retain for the present the power of removing any of them, either for the substitution of others or for my own occasional use ; but if the collections are found serviceable in the form ultimately proposed for them, and the system of teaching in accordance with which they have been arranged is sanctioned by the approval of the University, and recognized as a part of its educational curriculum, the entire series of examples would remain at the disposal of the University authorities. In the event of my death I mean them to be so left, in their present form ; left, that is to say, to the University, if it accept them on the condition of not altering their arrangement. I do not speak of them in my will ; if this public statement of my intention be not clear enough to stand in law, it may fall, and I shall not disturb myself ("Instructions in the Preliminary Exercises Arranged for the Lower Drawing School," 1873, pp. 2, 3).

Unfortunately, Mr. Ruskin parted from the University in anger, as we shall presently see, and the Drawing School has been considerably dismantled since the above passage was written. The only notable additions are a water-colour copy of Carpaccio's "St. Ursula's Dream," * and some copies made for Mr. Ruskin, by Mr. Fairfax Murray, from frescoes by Botticelli.

But far more curious and important than the works of art hung on the walls of the Drawing School are the collections contained in the cabinets arranged round the room. The construction of these cabinets is unique and deserves a word of explanation. They are of polished mahogany, and externally resemble somewhat a set of office washing-stands. Each of them holds either twelve or twenty-five drawings. The drawings are all framed—some in plain oak frames, others in a gilt beading of Mr.

* Fully described, and often referred to, in "Fors;" *e.g.*, 1872, xx. p. 13; 1876, pp. 329, 340, 350, 357, 381; 1878, p. 182. See also Appendix II. to this book, p. 249. It used sometimes to be an Oxford pleasantry to ask of diligent attendants at Mr. Ruskin's Lectures what new "greatest painter in the world" the Professor had discovered that day. The earliest reference to Carpaccio as "consummate" occurred, I believe, in his 1872 Lectures ("Ariadne Florentina," p. 94).

Severn's design *—and each frame fits into a
groove, an ivory label giving the number, and
a small leather strap for taking out being fitted
to one side of the frame. The contrivance
combines in an ingenious way security from
exposure to light and dust with handiness for
reference. The main collections are three in
number, entitled respectively (1) the Standard,
or Reference Series, (2) the Educational Series,
and (3) the Rudimentary Series. Some account
of the meaning of these several titles will be
given presently. Speaking of them generally,
one notes—first and last—that they are all alike
strictly and essentially educational. The historical significance or artistic quality in each
specimen is what is thought of, not its artistic
finish or material value. Hence that quaint
unexpectedness which has been noticed as
characteristic of Mr. Ruskin's lectures meets
one at almost every turn in these collections.
" Priceless " Turner drawings are arranged side
by side with coloured prints from old books
of travels. Exquisite studies from nature by

* This design, easily recognized when once seen, often
enables one to identify as having once belonged to Mr.
Ruskin drawings on view in salerooms or exhibitions,

Mr. Ruskin and his assistants keep company
with faded photographs. One passes from early
"states" of choice engravings to common
prints from cheap magazines. One soon finds,
nevertheless, that each specimen sufficiently fulfils its special purpose; and any curators or
committees who are organizing educational collections of fine art upon limited resources would
find a visit to the Ruskin Drawing School of
great interest. To the casual visitor the sudden
contrasts in the collections will be perhaps their
principal charm. If there are pleasures of
desultory picture-seeing as well as "pleasures
of desultory reading," the Ruskin Drawing
School—in spite of its elaborate systems—is
the place to enjoy them.

To offer guidance to a desultory reader is
absurd; and most desultory visitors will prefer
to browse upon the Ruskin collections at their
own sweet will. But it may be worth while
to note one or two points which will be found
of special interest by students of Mr. Ruskin's
work and writing. The first is the evidence,
continually recurring in each of the collections,
of the great labour spent by Mr. Ruskin upon
this part of his Professorial duties. And

herein I am speaking not only of the labour—
heavy though that must have been—involved in
collecting, arranging, cataloguing, and describing nearly nine hundred specimens, but also of
the amount of Mr. Ruskin's own handiwork contained in his cabinets. Of the drawings, some
hundred and seventy are by Mr. Ruskin's own
hand, and of these a very large number were
done expressly for his Oxford work. The
quantity of Mr. Ruskin's literary productions
is extraordinary; but his industry is amazing
when one takes count of his work as a draughtsman as well.* Moreover, the quality of his
artistic work is as fine as the quantity of it
is large. In many places in his writings Mr.
Ruskin has spoken, in terms which have sometimes seemed absurdly exaggerated, of the

* The secret of Mr. Ruskin's enormous output appears to
be his habit of early rising. "In summer," he says, "I
have been always at work, or out walking, by six o'clock,
usually awake by half-past four" ("Præterita," ii. 217).
And not only in summer; for I have heard him say that
much of his literary work has throughout his life been done
by morning candle-light. In one of his Oxford Lectures
Mr. Ruskin charged his pupils to remember that "all the
vital functions rise and set with the sun. . . . *Sol illuminatio
nostra est; Sol salus nostra ; Sol sapientia nostra*" ("Eagle's
Nest," § 104; see also "Two Paths," § 137; "Fors," 1873,
xxviii. p. 8; xxxiv. p. 31; 1875, p. 332).

amount of time spent by him upon rendering
details in his drawings.   In copying Veronese's
"Queen of Sheba" at Turin it took him six
weeks, he tells us, "to examine rightly two
figures," and one day he was "upwards of two
hours vainly trying to render with perfect accuracy the curves of two leaves of the brocaded
silk " ("Cambridge Inaugural Address," p. 12).
"I've been two whole days at work," he writes
at another time, "on the purple marsh orchis
alone" ("Fors," 1876, p. 172).   "No one has
the least notion," he complains, "of the quantity
of manual labour I have to go through to discharge my duty as a teacher of Art.   Look at
the frontispiece to Letter 20th ["Part of the
Chapel of St. Mary of the Thorn, Pisa "], which
is photographed from one of my architectural
sketches; and if you can draw, copy a bit of
it ; try merely the bead moulding with its
dentils, in the flat arch over the three small
ones, lowest on the left.   Then examine those
three small ones themselves.   You think I have
drawn them distorted, carelessly, I suppose.
No.   That distortion is essential to the Gothic
of the Pisan school ; and I measured every one
of the curves of those cusps on the spot, to

the tenth of an inch" (" Fors," 1875, p. 255).
Every one who examines Mr. Ruskin's handiwork in the Drawing School will soon form a
very clear notion of the quantity of manual
labour he went through in the discharge of his
duty as a teacher of Art.   That measuring of
curves to the tenth of an inch—conspicuous
enough already in the illustrations to the
" Stones of Venice " and in the " Examples of
Venetian Architecture "—is here seen applied
not to architecture only, but to every natural
form.   "If you can paint *one* leaf," says Mr.
Ruskin, in " Modern Painters " (vol. v., pt. vi.,
ch. 5, § 2), "you can paint the world."   Mr.
Ruskin lays no claim to be able to paint the
world, or indeed to any high rank as a painter
at all, but he has at least gone through loyal
apprenticeship in the painting of leaves.   Look,
for instance, at the exquisite care in his
" Peacock's Feather" (Reference Series, No.
114), with so much patient drawing of every
detail of form and every shadow of colour;
or in his " San Michele, Lucca " (Educ., 83);
or in the pieces of rolled gneiss (Educ., 276)
and of quartz (Educ., 277), showing with
the last degree of accuracy every vein and

weather-stain; or in the plumage of partridge (Rudim., 178). No matter what the subject may be, whether it be as lofty as the towers of Lucca or as lowly as the grass of the field, the same infinite patience is conspicuous everywhere. Not that Mr. Ruskin's work is inartistic from excess of finish, from painting what he knows by microscopic examination to be there rather than what he sees. In many cases, indeed, he does break this great artistic canon; but he does so deliberately, in order to make his specimens lessons in collateral science as well as examples of draughtsmanship. To Mr. Ruskin, as we have seen (p. 22), the teaching of Art is the teaching of everything. One great reason for the method adopted by him in teaching drawing (see above, p. 68) was, he says, that "it enables me to show you many things besides the art of drawing. Every exercise that I prepare for you will be either a portion of some important example of ancient art or of some natural object. However rudely or unsuccessfully you may draw it, you will nevertheless have learned what no words could have as forcibly or completely taught you, either respecting early art or organic structure; and I am thus certain that not a moment you spend attentively will be altogether wasted, and that, generally, you will be twice gainer by every effort." "The first principle," he says again, "of all I wish to enforce in my system here at Oxford is, that you shall never make a drawing, even for exercise, without proposing to learn some definite thing in doing so; nay, I will even go so far as to say that the drawing will never be made rightly unless the making it is subordinate to the gaining the piece of knowledge it is to represent and keep" ("Catalogue of the Rudimentary Series," p. 30).

Something of this double gain will accrue to the visitor who studies Mr. Ruskin's exquisitely delicate rendering of natural objects, and reads his discourses upon them in the catalogues. Especially interesting are the studies in flowers and leaves, with the system of mythological reference which Mr. Ruskin attaches to them (see, for instance, Educ., 4–15, and Rudim., 1, 227). But in many of Mr. Ruskin's drawings there is high artistic merit as well as scientific interest. Indeed, the best of them are chiefly remarkable for the success with which breadth of general effect is combined with wealth

F

of local detail. As examples in this kind the drawings of the Grand Canal at Venice (Ref., 66) and of the market-place of Abbeville (Ref., 61) may be mentioned. The latter, being a very elaborate study of one of Mr. Ruskin's "mother cities," is of especial interest. Many of the architectural drawings are valuable for their minutely faithful record of buildings since "restored." * It is in Mr. Ruskin's architectural sketches with the silver-point that his artistic gift is seen at its best, but the range of his studies is very wide. Besides the drawings of architecture and flowers already referred to, there are numerous studies of clouds, in water-colour (*e.g.*, Educ., 3); etchings from Turner drawings (*e.g.*, Educ., 101); many studies of animals (*e.g.*, Educ., 153–7); sketches of shells and fish, of Japanese enamels, of birds and

* Mr. Ruskin's sketch (Educ., 26) of the north porch of the west front of Amiens Cathedral, made in 1856, before its restoration, is a case in point. "The colour, in 1856, was," he says, "an exquisitely soft grey, touched with golden lichen; and the sheltered sculpture was as fresh as when first executed, only the exposed parts broken or mouldering into forms which made them more beautiful than if perfect. All is now destroyed, and even the sharp, pure rose moulding (of which hardly a petal was injured) cut to pieces, and, for the most part, replaced by a modern design."

beasts innumerable (see, especially, the " King-
fishers," Rudim., 201–5) ; many admirable landscapes, especially of Swiss scenes (*e.g.*, Educ.,
296, 297) ; and studies in heraldic design (*e.g.*,
Rudim., 8–11). It is amusing, after noticing
the evidence afforded by these cabinets of Mr.
Ruskin's long and various study of Art, to recall
the criticisms which have spoken of the Slade
Professor as " learned in many matters, and of
much experience at all, save his subject," and
as " talking for forty years of what he has never
done." *

* Mr. Ruskin refers to this criticism by anticipation in
the Preface to the third volume of "Modern Painters."
"There are two general principles to be kept in mind," he
says, "in examining the drawings of any writer on Art: the
first, that they ought at least to show such ordinary skill in
draughtsmanship as to prove that the writer knows *what*
the good qualities of drawing *are ;* the second, that they are
never to be expected to equal, in either execution or conception, the work of accomplished artists—for the simple
reason that in order to do *any*thing thoroughly well the
whole mind, and the whole available time, must be given
to that single art. . . . As, however, it is sometimes alleged,
by the opponents of my principles, that I have never *done*
*any*thing, it is proper that the reader should know exactly
the amount of work for which I am answerable in these
illustrations, &c." It is interesting to note that, though
many opponents of Mr. Ruskin's principles do allege (like
Mr. Whistler) that he has "never done anything," the latest
and (next to Mr. Whistler) the most violent opponent takes

To the student of Mr. Ruskin's books this collection of his drawings presents, however, many points of interest besides their artistic merit. Here, for one thing, are the original drawings for many of the plates with which every one is familiar in his published books. Readers of " Proserpina," in particular, will re-cognize many old friends in " Studies of Way-side Flowers;" and here, too, amongst others, is the " Purist Landscape," engraved in " Modern Painters" (Educ., 264, 269).

a precisely contrary line.   " In one respect only," says the *Edinburgh Review* (January 1888), "we are prepared to give Mr. Ruskin nearly unqualified admiration, namely, in regard to his own artistic work as far as it has gone : with the exception of those unhappy illustrations to the 'Seven Lamps,' his own drawing, of architecture especially, is ad-mirable.   When two or three of his own landscapes were exhibited some years ago in Bond Street, along with his Turners, our impression at the time was that they were equal to most of the Turner drawings in that collection ; at all events his drawings of portions of St. Mark's, exhibited more recently at the Society of Water-colours Exhibition, were of the highest class, and such as, indeed, of their kind, it would not be possible to surpass."   The reviewer might have added some reference to the admirable plates in "Modern Painters" of the Matterhorn and the Chamonix Aiguilles, "in which Mr. Ruskin (to quote an ex-President of the Alpine Club), to whom all mountain-lovers owe a debt of gratitude that can never be sufficiently acknow-ledged, set an example to future draughtsmen."

The drawings are rich, too, in autobiographical interest. The quality of *intimité* which has been noticed already as characteristic of Mr. Ruskin's Lectures, and which is the cause at once of his attraction and repulsion—attraction to those who, being in full sympathy with an author, like to be brought near to his personality; repulsion to those who, being without such sympathy, resent the personal note as "arrogant egotism"—this intimate quality is strongly marked in the collection of drawings at Oxford. Sometimes, indeed, Mr. Ruskin has framed actual leaves of his travelling diaries— diaries composed partly of written notes, partly of rough sketches. Thus the frame No. 172 in the Reference Series contains some leaves from the diary of an Italian tour in 1874.* The leaves are inserted for the sake of their architectural studies from the tombs of Roger the First and Frederick the Second at Palermo; but they are interspersed with travellers' notes such as the following: "Segni, west of line, quarter-hour past Velletri, worth stopping. Just past

* Some references to this tour, and especially to Palermo, will be found in "Ariadne Florentina," § 165. See also Appendix II. to this book, p. 238.

Segni Station, west portico of temple on hill, very important. Sparagla, magnificent hill town." Indeed, a devoted and diligent Ruskinian might almost compile an autobiography of the Master's wanderings from these Oxford drawings. Of his Venetian visits, and of the amount of work he did in careful architectural study, there is abundant evidence in several cabinets. Elsewhere we find him at Lucca (Educ., 83-85). A drawing of San Michele, containing much exquisite detail, is dated " 1845. J. R." This was the year of the visit to Lucca and Pisa which marked an epoch in Mr. Ruskin's mental and artistic development. " The inlaying of San Michele," he tells us, " opposed to Gothic *pierced* lace-work (which was all I cared for in Gothic at that time), and the fine and severe arcades of finely proportioned columns at San Frediano, doing stern duty under vertical walls, as opposed to Gothic shafts with no end, and buttresses with no bearing, struck me dumb with admiration and amazement " (Epilogue to small edition of " Modern Painters," vol. ii. ; see also " Præterita," xviii. and xix., and " Fors," 1874, p. 192). " Dumb with admiration and amazement," but not paralyzed ; and here, in these Oxford drawings, we have the first-fruits of that course of architectural study which (says Mr. Ruskin) "reduced under accurate law the vague enthusiasm of my childish taste, and has been ever since a method with me, guardian of all my other work in natural and moral philosophy." Another Italian city, connected with another epoch in Mr. Ruskin's mental history, is Assisi. It was there, in 1874, he tells us, that he "discovered a fallacy which had underlain all his Art teaching since the year 1858" ("Fors," 1877, p. 101)—the fallacy, namely, that "religious artists were weaker than irreligious." From that time forward Mr. Ruskin's critical estimates of the Italian painters were largely modified, and the visit to Assisi seems to have made, as was natural, a great impression on his mind. "Fors Clavigera" for 1874-5-6-7 is full of allusions to the sacristan's cell in which he worked, and he gave an annual gift of £25 to the monastery. Here (Ref., 297) is a sketch of the very cell, which is described at length in one letter (see "Fors," 1874, p. 223), and so often referred to in others. In like manner, one might follow the vein of autobiographical interest in many another sketch of foreign travel

—tracing Mr. Ruskin's course, as one turns over the contents of these cabinets, to Rheinfelden (Ref., 93), to Fribourg (Educ., 114), to Lucerne, (Educ., 116), or to "the Rock of Arona" (Ref., 92). But it is never for long that we find him away from his country home—studying the flowers and mosses of the wayside. Here, for instance (Educ., 11), is an exquisitely faithful drawing in colour of a wild strawberry plant, thus inscribed :—

> "The Rose of Demeter.*
> Springing in a cleft of her rocks.
> J. Ruskin. Brantwood, June, '73."

Still more interesting, perhaps, to those who are in sympathy with the author of "Modern Painters" is another drawing in the same cabinet (Educ., 6), a "study of a few blades of grass as they grew." "Examine for a minute, quietly,

---

* "I give the strawberry-blossom to Demeter because it is the prettiest type of the uncultured and motherly gifts of the earth. Also, I take the blossom as the kindest and usefullest representative of the Rose tribe, and in a sort the most central; for if I took Rosa Canina instead, it would not suggest the great groups of the potentillas and tormentillas; nor the relation to the anemone through the Dryas; but this strawberry-blossom expresses the place of all these, and yet is itself clearly a little white rose" ("Catalogue of the Educational Series," p. 30).

its narrow, sword-shaped strip of fluted green.
Nothing, as it seems, there, of notable goodness
or beauty. A very little strength, and a very
little tallness, and a few delicate long lines meeting in a point—not a perfect point neither, but
blunt and unfinished; by no means a creditable or apparently much-cared-for example of
Nature's workmanship; made, as it seems, only
to be trodden on to-day, and to-morrow to be cast
into the oven; and a little pale and hollow stalk,
feeble and flaccid, leading down to the dull brown
fibres of the roots. And yet, think of it well,
and judge whether, of all the gorgeous flowers
that beam in summer air, and of all strong and
goodly trees, pleasant to the eyes or good for
food—stately palm and pine, strong ash and
oak, scented citron, burdened vine—there be
any by man so deeply loved, by God so highly
graced, as that narrow point of feeble green.
. . . Consider what we owe merely to the mea-
dow grass, to the covering of the dark ground
by that glorious enamel, by the companies of
those soft, and countless, and peaceful spears.
. . . Go out, in the spring-time, among the
meadows that slope from the shores of the Swiss
lakes to the roots of their lower mountains.

There, mingled with the taller gentians and
the white narcissus, the grass grows deep and
free; and as you follow the winding mountain paths, beneath arching boughs all veiled
and dim with blossom—paths that for ever
droop and rise over the green banks and mounds,
sweeping down, in scented undulation, steep to
the blue water, studded here and there with
new-mown heaps, filling all the air with fainter
sweetness—look up towards the higher hills,
where the waves of everlasting green roll silently
into their long inlets among the shadows of the
pines; and we may, perhaps, at last know the
meaning of those quiet words of the Hundred
and forty-seventh Psalm, 'He maketh grass to
grow upon the mountains.'"

The contents of the Ruskin Drawing School
are not, however, "precious" only for the sake
of Mr. Ruskin himself. The specimens are
selected, as has been explained, for their appro-
priateness in an educational series; but they
include, by Mr. Ruskin's generosity, many engravings and drawings of great interest and
value in themselves. Among the former, Mr.
Ruskin notifies the woodcuts by Hans Burgkmair (Rudim., 26-38), as "entirely perfect

examples of execution with the pure black line."
But there are also several by Dürer, as well as
a curious photographic enlargement of a Madonna's head by him (Ref., 144), very instructive as bringing prominently before the student
the distinctive character of wood-cutting.   In
which connection it is interesting to find in an
adjacent cabinet the frame of cheap modern
woodcuts referred to by Mr. Ruskin in the "Art
of England" lectures, in which he maintained
that, "while no entirely beautiful thing can be
represented in a woodcut, every form of vul-
garity or unpleasantness can be given, to the
life."   In illustration of this proposition we
have here (Ref., 164) "a collection of woodcuts
out of a scientific survey of South America, presenting collectively, in designs ignorantly drawn
and vilely engraved, yet with the peculiar advantage belonging to the cheap woodcut, whatever, through that fourth part of the round
world from Mexico to Patagonia, can be found
of savage, sordid, vicious, or ridiculous in
humanity" ("Art of England," p. 169).   After
which it will be well, perhaps, to turn for relief
to some of Dürer's engravings again (*e.g.*, Educ.,
74, 75), which " show his power over human

character and expression, and are full of suggestions of thought."

Passing next from engravings to copies and transcripts from natural forms, we shall come across a great deal of very beautiful work by Mr. Ruskin's assistant, the late Arthur Burgess. His work meets us, indeed, in nearly every cabinet, and we cannot, therefore, notice it in detail. The reader may be referred to the general account which Mr. Ruskin recently gave of his friend in the "Century Guild Hobby-Horse" (vol. ii., 46–53). "During the years," he says, "when I was lecturing, or arranging the examples in my schools, Mr. Burgess was engaged at fixed salary, executing either the woodcuts necessary to illustrate my lectures, or drawings to take permanent place in the school examples. So far as I was able to continue 'Proserpina,' the woodcuts were always executed by him; and indeed I was wholly dependent on his assistance for the effectual illustrations of my most useful books. Especially those in 'Ariadne Florentina' and 'Aratra Pentelici' are unequalled, whether in precision of facsimile or the legitimate use of the various methods of wood-engraving according to his own judgment."

In addition to this work, Mr. Burgess had before, in 1869, been to Verona with Mr. Ruskin,
studying the Scala tombs, and of these drawings
also many examples are to be seen in the Educational Series : " He drew," says Mr. Ruskin,
" as architecture had never been drawn before."
Another series of architectural drawings of great
interest, historical as well as artistic, are those
by another of Mr. Ruskin's assistants—the late
Mr. Bunney.* The drawings of Lucca and
Verona (Ref., 76–83) are good examples of
" the unwearied care and perseverance " of that
conscientious artist. Mr. Ruskin's affection for
Prout and W. Hunt is well known, and his Drawing School is rich in examples by both those
painters. Drawings by Prout will be found in
Educ., 111, 129, 133–35, and in Rudim., 25,
85, 136, 137; drawings by Hunt in Educ.,
168, 192, 213; and in Rudim., 59, 60, 179, 180.
Amongst the Prouts special attention may be
called to the drawing of Mayence (Rudim., 136),
both as an admirable example of his fine pencil-

* An interesting and sympathetic memoir of Mr. Bunney,
from the pen of Mr. A. Wedderburn ("An Oxford Pupil"),
was prefixed to the "Catalogue of the Exhibition held at
the Fine Art Society in 1882."

work, and as a record of a singularly picturesque scene now swept away by modern improvements. Mr. Ruskin has written so much, in
so many places, about " old William Hunt " that
it is unnecessary to refer to his drawings here.
It may be interesting, however, to mention more
particularly a study of " Peach and Grapes "
(Educ., 213), which Mr. Ruskin contrasts, in
virtue of its " general look of greengrocery and
character of rustic simplicity," with the grave
refinement of the Italian designers illustrated
elsewhere in the same series. " Generally
speaking," adds Mr. Ruskin, " you will find our
best modern art has something of this quality
—it looks as if done by peasants or untrained
persons, while good Italian work is visibly by
accomplished gentlemen. . . . 'I like to see a
thing *fudged* out,' said William Hunt once to
me. Yes; but to see it felt out, and known,
both out and in, is better still." All the Prout
and Hunt drawings in these cabinets have been
presented to the University by Mr. Ruskin, who
has further enriched them with several drawings
by Turner. Of these the most important are
Nos. 2 and 3 in the Reference Series. Speaking,
in his first lecture at Oxford, of " the instinctive

love of landscape" which is characteristic of
English art, Mr. Ruskin reminded his hearers
that "a nation is only worthy of the soil and
the scenes that it has inherited when, by all its
acts and arts, it is making them more lovely
for its children." The first three specimens
selected for the Reference Series were, therefore, of landscape scenes. The first—"Brignal
Banks, on the Greta, near Rokeby"—is an engraving only (the original drawing by Turner
having been destroyed by fire), but is "a perfect type of the loveliest English scenery,
touched by imaginative associations." The
second example—the "Junction of the Greta
and Tees"—is a real drawing by Turner—"Of
all I have," said Mr. Ruskin, "the one I had
least mind to part with. It is," he added, "a
faultless example of Turner's work at the time
when it is most exemplary."

The third Turner—a scene on the Loire,
never engraved—is an introduction to the Loire
Series, previously presented by Mr. Ruskin to
the University galleries. "Though small, it
is," he says, "very precious, being a faultless
and, I believe, unsurpassable example of water-
colour painting." As for its place in the

Reference Series, it was "chosen in further illustration of the pensiveness of the chiaroscurist
school. It is painted wholly in solid colour, as
No. 2 is painted wholly in transparent; and
the two drawings together show the complete
management of colours soluble in water or thin
liquid of any kind" (Oxford "Lectures on
Art," § 25, "Catalogue of the Reference Series,"
pp. 2-4). In the Rudimentary Series (No.
300) is another Turner drawing, to which, in a
different way, Mr. Ruskin attaches special importance. This is a "Pen and Sepia Sketch
for Unpublished Plate of Liber Studiorum"—
"unique among Turner's sepia sketches for its
grace and ease." These are the most important
Turner drawings in the collection, but there are
many others of considerable, though slighter,
value. Especially interesting, as showing the
detailed drawing which Turner put into a sketch
before laying on colour, is an unfinished study of
a ruined abbey (Educ., 102)—"a witness to you,
once for all," says Mr. Ruskin, "of the right
way to work: doing nothing without clearly
formed intention, nothing in a hurry, nothing
more wrong than you can help; all as tenderly
as you can, all as instantly as you can; all

thoughtfully, and nothing mechanically." Farther on, in the same series, are three pencil
sketches (the last with colour begun) by Turner
(Educ., 126–128); the first, an early sketch and
rough; the second, later and full of detail; the
third, especially interesting for an exquisitely
rendered thistle in the foreground. In the same
cabinet are several of Turner's architectural
sketches; in another are studies of fish, birds,
and cattle (Educ., 181–3, 185); and in the last
one, a few sketches of clouds and hills (Educ.,
292, 293, 300). These are of the same general
character as the numerous studies in the National
Gallery. A further batch of Turner's drawings
meets us in the Rudimentary Series. Very interesting, as a specimen of work not common
with Turner, is the Farnley interior (Rudim.,
14), a careful study of armour and *bric-à-brac.*
This is signed "Turner, R.A., 1815." Some
other drawings in these series were included in
the exhibition held at the Fine Art Society's
galleries in 1878, and a simple reference to
those numbers (126–31) will therefore suffice
here. In the cabinet containing these drawings
there are also some of the wonderful copies of
Turner executed for Mr. Ruskin by Mr. William

Ward* (145–149). The Turner drawings described above are, it should be remembered, entirely distinct from the other series of sixty-one drawings which were presented by Mr. Ruskin to Oxford some years before, and which hang in the University galleries above the Drawing School. † Furthermore, the Trustees of the

* Of these copies Professor Ruskin says, "They are executed with extreme care, under my own eye, by the draughtsman trained by me for the purpose, Mr. Ward. Everything that can be learned from the smaller works of Turner may be as securely learned from these drawings. I have been more than once in doubt, seeing original and copy together, which was which, and I think them about the best works that can now be obtained for a moderate price, representing the authoritative forms of art in landscape."—*Catalogue of the Fine Art Department, Harvard University.*

† Mr. Ruskin's gifts, to various institutions, of Turner drawings alone, must represent a money value of several thousand pounds. (Some years ago he assessed his gifts to Oxford and "St. George" at £15,000.) The series of Turners given to the Oxford University galleries is especially fine. Nor was the gift a money sacrifice only. "When," he says somewhere, incidentally, "I gave away my Loire series of Turner drawings to Oxford, I thought I was rational enough to enjoy them as much in the University gallery as in my own study. But not at all! I find I can't bear to look at them in the gallery, because they are 'mine' no more." Elsewhere he makes lighter of the gift. "It is a woeful fault of this collection of mine, considered as illustrative of his life, that there are no

National Gallery have placed on loan in the same galleries a large number of sketches from those bequeathed to the nation; * so that the collection of Turner drawings and sketches at Oxford is now second, in importance and interest, only to that at the National Gallery itself.

Finally, we must not forget to mention among the treasures of the Ruskin School several drawings by distinguished living artists. Some studies of flowers by Mr. A. McWhirter (Educ., 258–61) and landscapes by Mr. A. Goodwin (Rudim., 139–42) are well worth looking at. There is a very interesting pencil drawing of a lemon tree by Sir Frederick Leighton, done at Capri, and signed "L. 59." The delicacy with which every piece of fruit and foliage is rendered is unsurpassable.   It is an example which

---

Venetian sketches in it. I gave all I had to Cambridge and Oxford, not generously, but because to think of Venice now is mere misery to me" (Notes on his "Drawings by Turner," p. 105). The Cambridge gift consisted of twenty-five Turner drawings, again very choice specimens, to the Fitzwilliam Museum.

* The loan comprises two hundred and fifty drawings, arranged by Mr. Ruskin into twenty-five series, and eight sketch-books.

"determines without appeal," says Mr. Ruskin, "the question respecting necessity of delineation as the first skill of a painter. Of all our present masters, Sir Frederick Leighton delights most in softly blended colours, and his ideal of beauty is more nearly that of Correggio than any seen since Correggio's time. But you see by what precision of terminal outline he at first restrained, and exalted, his gift of beautiful *vaghezza*" ("The Art of England," pp. 97–8). Equally exemplary are the pencil drawings of Mr. Burne-Jones. "His outline," said Mr. Ruskin, in the same course of lectures (p. 65), "is the purest and quietest that is possible to the pencil. Nearly all other masters accentuate falsely, or in some places, as Richter, add shadows which are more or less conventional; but an outline by Burne-Jones is as pure as the lines of engraving on an Etruscan mirror, and I placed the series of drawings from the story of Psyche in your school as faultlessly exemplary in this kind. Whether pleasing or displeasing to your taste, they are entirely masterful; and it is only by trying to copy these or other such outlines that you will fully feel the grandeur of action in the moving hand,

tranquil and swift as a hawk's flight, and never
allowing a vulgar tremor or a momentary impulse to impair its precision or disturb its
serenity." The Psyche drawings referred to in
this passage are to be found in the Educational
Series, Nos. 64–72, & 223. The last one is particularly noted by Mr. Ruskin, in his catalogue,
as the best possible example of " refinement in
design obtained by perfectly simple and firm
equality of outline, and of the decorative placing
and arranging of every accessory. There is not
a cluster of grass, nor are there two leaves set
side by side, throughout the drawing, without
perfectly invented decorative relation to each
other." There are also, by Mr. Burne-Jones,
a "Study for Head of Danae" (Educ., 224)
and two studies from Tintoret (Educ., 225, and
Rudim., 113). Lastly, in a separate cabinet are
" XII. Drawings by Francesca Alexander, given
to Oxford by John Ruskin, 1883." These are
the original drawings for the " Roadside Songs
of Tuscany," by the American lady Miss
Francesca Alexander, to whose art gift Mr.
Ruskin has of late years paid the highest tri-
butes, and whose drawings have been placed
in his school "to be standards of method, in

drawing from the life, to students capable of a determined industry." *

The desultory account, now completed, of the drawings in Mr. Ruskin's School, will have given the reader some idea of the wealth of interest to be found in its cabinets. But the visitor who wishes to derive from them their full educational value should examine them in the order and upon the system devised by Mr. Ruskin for his pupils. In order to understand this system, it is necessary to remember, in the first place, the double purpose which Mr. Ruskin had in view. His principal object was to establish in the University a School of Criticism; his second, to establish a School of Art. With the former object in view, he collected the Standard or Reference Series of examples; with the latter object in view, the Educational and the Rudimentary Series. The scope of the former series is sufficiently indicated by its

* Miss Alexander's graceful sketches of the Tuscan peasantry—both in pen-drawing and in writing—will be familiar to many readers in "The Story of Ida," "The Roadside Songs of Tuscany," and "Christ's Folk in the Apennine." An interesting description of the lady herself was recently published in the New York *Critic* and summarized in the *Pall Mall Gazette* (May 13th, 1887).

title; it was to be a series of "*standards* to
which you may at once *refer* on any question-
able point, and by the study of which you may
gradually attain an instinctive sense of right,
which will afterwards be liable to no serious
error. . . . The real utility of the series will
depend on its restricted extent—on the severe
exclusion of all second-rate, superfluous, or even
attractively varied examples—and on the con-
fining the students' attention to a few types of
what is insuperably good" (Oxford "Lectures on
Art," § 21).   This Standard Series was originally intended by Mr. Ruskin to comprise four
sections of a hundred pieces each—illustrating,
severally, (1) the schools of painting in general,
(2) the sculpture and allied arts of the Gothic
races, (3) the sculpture and allied arts of the
Greeks, and (4) the special skill of modern times.
This, however, remains "a counsel of perfection."   Mr. Ruskin has always been one of
those (to use a vulgar but expressive phrase)
whose "eyes are bigger than their stomachs."
All that he actually arranged was the first of the
four sections above enumerated, and even there
he only reached half-way through his task.
The "schools of painting in general" were, in

their turn, to have been subdivided into two
sections, of fifty each, containing severally, (*a*)
standards for illustration of *methods*, (*b*) forms
of *thought* in Christian painting.   It is the first
of these two sub-sections only which got itself
arranged.   It is to be found in the pieces numbered 1–50, contained in the first two of the
large cabinets which occupy the alcove of
the Drawing School.   A rough analysis of
their contents, with occasional references to
Mr. Ruskin's lectures, etc., is given on pp.
106, 107.

Here, as above explained, the so-called "Standard Series" breaks off; the remaining large
cabinets, placed in the alcove, contain the
" Reference Series," which is described by Mr.
Ruskin as being of "quite mixed character."
There are, moreover, a great many blanks in it ;
but although arranged in no very systematic
order, these cabinets cover to a large extent the
second and third groups mentioned above (see
p. 103), namely, the art of the Gothic races and
of the Greeks respectively.   Thus they include
(1) a large number of specimens of " the architecture which depends chiefly for its effect on
the sculpture or colouring of surfaces, as opposed

to that which depends on construction or proportion of forms," and (2) several designs from
vases, etc., illustrative of the essential features
of Greek Art.   But it would be useless to look
for systematic arrangement where none was
intended.   The Reference Series was intended
for miscellaneous reference only.   It should
be studied in connection with Mr. Ruskin's
lectures.   In these lectures he illustrated his
arguments point by point—historical, moral, or
technical—by reference to actual examples of
art : this Reference Series was to be the gradually accumulated collection of such examples,
and in the Oxford "Lectures on Art" the reader
will find it continually referred to in this way.

With the Educational and the Rudimentary
Series, which now remain to be explained, the
case is different.   These collections were arranged with a view rather to use in a working
School of Art than for reference in critical lectures.   The Educational Series was the first to
be arranged, and was intended for the comparatively mature University students whom Mr.
Ruskin originally hoped to attract.   It soon,
however, became evident that Mr. Ruskin's
pupils would be mainly young ladies, and for

THE "STANDARD SERIES:" NOS. 1-50.

	Examples of—	Artists and Pictures.	Referred to in
1-3	Imaginative Landscape	Turner: "Yorkshire" and "Loire"	"Eagle's Nest," § 70. Oxford "Lectures on Art," §§ 25, 170.
4	Spirit of Labour allied thereto	Dürer's "Melancholia"	"Modern Painters," vol. v., part ix., chap. iv., § 17-19.
5	Perfection in Painting	Bellini's "Madonna and Saints"	"Standard Catalogue," p. 6.
6	The Art of Illumination	St. Louis's Psalter	Ib., p. 8.
7		Page of Service Book	
8	Perfect Delineation by School of Colour	Cima's "St. John the Baptist"	Oxford "Lectures on Art," § 150.
9	Perfect Delineation by School of Chiaroscuro	Dürer's "Knight and Death"	See under 4 above, and "Ariadne Florentina," *passim.*
10		,, "Adam and Eve"	
11	Grace in Delineation	Leonardo's "Vierge aux Rochers"	See "Handbook to the National Gallery," No. 1,093.
12		,, "Studies of Heads"	
13	Chalk Drawing	Correggio's "Assumption" (sketch)	"Standard Catalogue," pp. 10, 11. "Seven Lamps," chap. ii., § 15.
14		Correggio: Studies	
15		Raphael's "Noah"	
16		,, "Sposalizio"	"Standard Catalogue," pp. 11-14; and see references to Mr. Ruskin on Raphael, collected in "Handbook to the National Gallery," under No. 1,171.
17	Academical Grace: Raphaelesque.	,, "Theology"	
18		,, "Justice"	
19		,, "Poetry"	
20		,, "Parnassus"	

No.		Reference
21	⎫ Realism : Venetian School · ⎨ Bonifazio's "Sebastian" · ⎬ Tintoret's "Graces" · ⎩ Titian's "Madonna."	"Standard Catalogue," p. 14.
22		"Michael Angelo and Tintoret, p. 29."
23	(Not catalogued.)	
24–34		
35	⎫ Schools of Delineation · Mantegna : "Martyrdom of St. James."	"Standard Catalogue," p. 16.
36	Mantegna : Portrait	
37	Bellini and Raphael : Madonnas	"Lectures on Art," § 183.
38	Van Eyck ⎫	
39	Holbein ⎬ Examples of.	
40	⎩ Vandyck's "Prince of Savoy"	
41	" "Daughter of Charles I."	"Modern Painters," vol. v., part ix, chap. vii., § 23 n.
42	Reynolds's "English Girl" ·	"Lectures on Art," § 183.
43	The preceding examples show perfect skill in the School of Delineation (the drawing being wrought with the point of the brush). These are examples of the School of Colour (the brush being used broadly). See Oxford "Lectures on Art," Lect. V.	
44	" "English Gentleman."	
45	Velasquez : "Margaret of Austria."	
46	" "Portrait of a Knight."	
47	Titian : "Charles V. on Horseback."	
48	" "Charles V. with Dog."	
49	Tintoret (example not chosen).	
50	" "Two Senators and the Paradise"	"Michael Angelo and Tintoret," passim.

their benefit the Rudimentary Series was next
arranged. The two series are thus nearly
parallel, the latter being slightly more elementary than the former. Each series consists of
twelve cabinets, and each cabinet contains (or
should contain) twenty-five specimens. The
general arrangement of the cabinets is shown
on p. 109.

In the following analysis some description is
given of the specimens selected, and of the
method of their arrangement. I go thus into
detail because Mr. Ruskin's Drawing School
may well, I think, afford valuable hints for the
arrangement of school museums and elementary
Art galleries—such as should exist in every
town, if not in every school.

The Educational Series.

1. *Introductory : Exercises in Flowers.*

These are elementary exercises in outline and flat-
tint. But Mr. Ruskin designedly makes them
exercises also in elementary botany and mytho-
logy. He selects, for copying, sketches of the
tribes of flowers " which have had the strongest
influence on the human mind in all ages "—*e.g.*,
the amaryllids (Christ's "lily of the field"), the
irids (the *ion* of Ionia and the fleur-de-lis of

SCHEME OF THE "EDUCATIONAL" AND THE "RUDIMENTARY" SERIES.

EDUCATIONAL.	RUDIMENTARY.
1. Introductory : Exercises in Flowers.	1. Heraldry.
2. Elementary Greek Design.	2. Heraldry.
3. Northern Gothic.	3. Greek and Mediæval Design.
4. Italian Gothic.	4. Gothic Design.
5. Elementary Landscape.	5. Revived Classical Design.
6. Advanced Landscape.	6. Landscape.
7. } Animals in Sculpture and Painting.	7. Landscape.
8. }	8. Birds.
9. Connection between Decorative and Realistic Design.	9. Birds.
10. Etching, Engraving, and Outline Drawing.	10. Grasses and Foreground Plants.
11. Foliage.	11. Tree-foliage.
12. Rocks, Water, and Clouds.	12. Exercises in Tree-drawing.

Christian Europe), the asphodels (the Greek
flower of immortality), and the lilies (the lily of
the Annunciation).

The actual examples here are mostly drawings by
Mr. Ruskin or his assistant.

II. *Elementary Greek Design.*

Examples of architecture, vase-painting, etc., illustrative of the strictness of Greek design. This
cabinet includes engravings of the Parthenon
and the Erechtheium, sketches of the foliage on
Greek coins, and engravings of mythological
designs on Greek vases.

III. *Northern Gothic Design:* (1) *in Architecture,*
(2) *in its Resultant Art.*

The object of this cabinet is to illustrate "the
course of the arts in the North of Europe, from
the development of their first perfect elementary
school of round-arched architecture to the consummate work of German artists in the sixteenth
century."

The examples are arranged in the following order:—
Architecture: (1) the primary form of ecclesiastical architecture—photograph of Norman chapel
near Abbeville ; (2) a central type of pure
Gothic sculpture—photograph of Chartres Cathedral ; (3) "a quite balanced example of perfect
Gothic, uniting all its elements (figure-sculptures,
diaper surface-ornament, foliation, absolute simplicity of mechanical structure in gable and
arch)" — photograph of small north door of
Notre Dame ; (4) characteristic English Gothic,
when it separated itself from German and

French—Prout's drawings of York Minster and
of the chapel on the bridge of Wakefield ; (5)
"the grandest achievement of Gothic architectural science"—photograph of the spire of Stras-
burg Cathedral ; (6) the relation of Late Gothic
to domestic life—photographs of Hôtel Bourg-
theroude, Rouen, and of wooden houses at
Abbeville. *Resultant Art:* engravings from
Dürer and Holbein, etc.

IV. *Italian Gothic Design :* (1) *in Architecture,* (2) *in
its Resultant Art.*

The corresponding object of this cabinet is to
illustrate "the course of Southern (that is to say,
essentially of Italian) Art, from its first asser-
tion of itself as a distinct style in the thirteenth
century to its perfect results in the sixteenth."
The last cabinet illustrated also, in the work of
Holbein and Dürer, the intellectual power in the
North which led to the Reformation. This "ex-
hibits the full force of pure Catholicism in Italy,
and of the highest Christian Art, which is its
expression."

The examples given are—of *Architecture,* several
drawings by Mr. Ruskin from Verona, Lucca,
Como, Padua, and Venice (also a photograph of
the famous Colleone statue) ; of *Resultant Art,*
photographs of Filippo Lippi's "Annunciation"
and "Nativity" at Florence, and Luini's "Adora-
tion of the Magi."

V. & VI. *Landscape.*

The examples here are not arranged on any easily
discernible system, Mr. Ruskin being guided, no

doubt, in their selection, by his own preferences and by his possession of Turner drawings. The landscape examples begin with an etching from Turner's "Banks of the Loire" (in the Oxford University Galleries), "because it illustrates the chief motive in sentiment with Turner, and with all the great landscapists—rest, in clear air and by sweet waters, after the day's due labour. (Compare the saw left in the wood, here, with the plough in the last vignette to Rogers's poems, 'Datur hora quieti.')"

VII. & VIII. *Elementary Zoology.*

"Illustrations of the treatment of animal form by the higher methods of sculpture and painting." Most of the examples here are drawings by Turner, Hunt, and Mr. Ruskin. But the following studies or photographs from old masters, etc., are included : "Pulpit at Siena," with supporting animals : Dürer's "St. Jerome and Lion ;" "The Lion of St. Mark's ;" Carpaccio's "Red Parrot" (from the "St. George" Series) ; * and Giovanni Pisano's "Eagle" at Pisa.

* "A beautiful scarlet—'parrot' (must we call him ?), conspicuously mumbling at a violet flower under the steps ; him also—finding him the scarletest and mumblingest parrot I had ever seen—I tried to paint, in 1872, for the Natural History Schools of Oxford — perhaps a new species, or extinct old one, to immortalise Carpaccio's name and mine. When all the imaginative arts shall be known no more, perhaps in Darwinian Museums, this scarlet *Epops Carpaccii* may preserve our fame" ("St. Mark's Rest," "The Shrine of the Slaves," p. 9). The "Epops Carpaccii" is Educ., 161.

IX. *Connection between Decorative and Realistic Design.*

"Many of the photographs and engravings in the first eight cabinets are for study only, not for copying; but all in the last four are intended for exact guidance in practice." The examples in this cabinet include thirteenth and fourteenth century missals, the sculpture on the angles of the Ducal Palace, and Mr. Burne-Jones's Psyche drawings.

X. *Etching, Engraving, and Outline Drawing.*

The models selected by Mr. Ruskin for these branches of art are Holbein, Dürer, Leonardo, and Turner; whilst Rembrandt's "Angels Appearing to the Shepherds" is given as "an example of every kind of badness."

XI. *Foliage.*

Here, again, are several engravings from Turner ("Florence from Fiesole," "Buckfastleigh," "Aske Hall," "Rokeby," "Kirkby Lonsdale"); also photographs or sketches from Botticelli (" Spring") and Raphael (" Madonna of the Tribune").

XII. *Rocks, Water, and Clouds.*

Here the examples are almost entirely of Turner's work. Mr. Ruskin was able to include many originals, and has added some of his own studies; but any reader of "Modern Painters" will know what engravings or photographs from Turner would best illustrate the subject.

H

THE RUDIMENTARY SERIES.

This series follows so closely the lines of the Educational that it does not seem worth while to describe it in detail. The following points may, however, serve as supplementary suggestions for the formation of any similar collection of examples. Under Division I., above, Hans Burgkmair's woodcuts representing the Triumph of Maximilian I., and photographs or sketches of many royal shields and tombs, are added. Under Divisions VII. and VIII. the prints of Gould's "English Ornithology" are given : "Entire dependence may be placed," says Mr. Ruskin, "on their accuracy of representation, and I believe even a few examples will be greatly useful in exciting the interest of the younger students in ornithology, and especially in the living birds." Some plates from Curacci's " Natural History " and Le Vaillant's " Birds of Paradise " are also given. The examples of Grasser, etc., are taken from " Floræ Danicæ" and Mr. Loudon's " Bulbous Plants."

The inventory of the Ruskin Drawing School which has now been completed will, I hope, have given the reader some idea of its curious and unique interest. It is interesting as things are; but if all had gone well with Mr. Ruskin, it would have been more interesting still, and even now it might be made far more interesting than it is. In its present condition the Drawing School, on its exhibition side, is little more than an outline. There is enough to show what Mr. Ruskin intended to make of it, but his intentions are to a large extent left unfulfilled. The explanatory catalogues remain half unwritten, and the cabinets are left either imperfectly filled or altogether empty. " I must myself," he wrote in 1870, "make several more careful drawings, to take the place of hurried ones; and, especially in the supplementary examples of rock and tree drawing, some of the engravings will be ultimately changed or have drawings put in their place." "The greater number of examples I shall choose," he said, in his first lecture at Oxford, "will not at first be costly. But in process of time I have good hope that assistance will be given me by the English public in making the series here no less splendid than serviceable." During his first tenure of the Slade Professorship these purposes steadily advanced, though most of the "splendid" specimens added to the collections were the result, I fancy, of Mr. Ruskin's unaided generosity. When he resumed the Professorship in 1883 he resumed also his work upon the Drawing School. A rearrangement of the specimens was begun, and Mr. Ruskin placed many fresh treasures at the service of his pupils. In April, 1885, however, Mr. Ruskin abruptly resigned his post, and resigned it —as will be seen from the following letter of explanation—in bitterness and vexation of spirit :—

"MR. RUSKIN AND THE SLADE PROFESSORSHIP.

"*To the Editor of the* Pall Mall Gazette.

"SIR,—By mischance I have not till to-day seen your kindly meant paragraphs on my resignation of the Slade Professorship at Oxford. Yet permit me at once to correct the impression under which they were written. Whatever may be my failure in energy or ability, the best I could yet do was wholly at the service of Oxford ; nor would any other designs or supposed duties have interfered for a moment with the perfectly manifest duty of teaching in Oxford as much Art as she gave her students time to learn. I meant to die in my harness there, and my resignation was placed in the Vice-Chancellor's hands on the Monday following the vote endowing vivisection in the University, solely in consequence of that vote, with distinct statement to the Vice-Chancellor, intended to be read in Convocation, of its being so. This statement I repeated in a letter intended for publication in the *University Gazette*, and sent to its office a fortnight since. Neither of these letters, so far as I know, has yet been made public. It is sufficient proof, however, how far it was contrary to my purpose to retire from the Slade Professorship, that

I applied in March of last year for a grant to build a
well-lighted room for the undergraduates, apart from
the obscure and inconvenient Ruskin School ; and to
purchase for its furniture the two Yorkshire drawings by
Turner of " Crook of Lune " and " Kirkby Lonsdale "—
grants instantly refused on the plea of the University's
being in debt.

"I am, Sir, your obedient servant,

"JOHN RUSKIN.

" BRANTWOOD, *April* 24*th*, 1885."

The refusal of the University to meet Mr.
Ruskin's lavish generosity in any corresponding
spirit undoubtedly had something to do with his
resignation.*   But whatever may have been the

---

* I had some conversation with Mr. Ruskin on this subject a few months afterwards.   "Double motives," he said,
"are very useful things ; you can do a thing for two that
you could not do for one."   The vivisection vote was perhaps the principal motive of his resignation ; but *chagrin* at
what he thought the niggardliness of the University was a
secondary one.   Immediately on resuming the Professorship in 1883, he had given expression to this grievance.
"He noticed in his lecture yesterday," said the *Pall Mall
Gazette*, Nov. 8th, 1883, "as characteristic of the scientific
tendencies of the present day, that while the University
will spend £100,000 or even £150,000 in decorating, in a
style as incorrect as it is un-English, rooms for the torture
of her students, she gives her art-workers nothing better
than a cellar to draw in, and her Art Professor no other
place for the storage of his models than a corner of his
private office in the gallery."   Mr. Ruskin might have added

cause, the fact is certain that he parted from his old University in anger. He removed from the Drawing School most of such interesting specimens as were not included in his previous deed of gift, and it is unlikely—especially now that the Ruskin Museum at Sheffield has assumed definite shape—that they will ever be restored. The contemplated rearrangement was abandoned, and the specimens that remained were put back into their old places—with the result that there are a great many gaps in most of the cabinets.

It is a thousand pities that something should not be done to bring the collections into a more completed order, and to make them more generally useful. I do not doubt that the University

what must have occurred to most of his closely packed and half-stifled audience, that it was a pity the Slade Professor had no better place to lecture in than the theatre of the museum. "Meanwhile the study of figure drawing set on foot by Mr. Richmond is impossible," Mr. Ruskin said, "until the University makes the 'indispensable additions' to the Taylorian buildings." Recently, I may add, the University has made considerable enlargements to its galleries, and it was proposed to accommodate the Ruskin Drawing School in one of the new rooms. It has been decided, however, to retain the *genius loci*, and leave it in its original quarters, the chief inconvenience of which is that the room is lighted entirely from the east.

had good reasons for refusing the considerable expenditure for which Mr. Ruskin asked. But having in its possession collections of great value, it is surely false economy to grudge the trifling expenditure necessary to make those possessions capable of yielding their full return in usefulness. The University galleries themselves (and not the Ruskin Drawing School only) stand in need of overhauling—there is not even so much as a complete catalogue of the pictures, and the proper course, therefore, would seem to be to appoint some one to the duty of organizing and supervising both collections.* The work which such an expert might do in the Ruskin Drawing School is very simple, but very useful. The Standard Series should be revised and completed on the general lines laid down by Mr. Ruskin. The Educational and Rudimentary Series should be amalgamated. An explanatory and descriptive catalogue should then be prepared, in the compilation of which Mr.

* At Cambridge, Mr. Middleton, the Slade Professor, has lately been appointed Curator also of the University galleries. The Curators of the University Galleries at Oxford are a large board. The Keeper is Mr. Macdonald, whose work, however, is already too heavy to leave him time for any such task of reorganization as is suggested above.

Ruskin's own catalogues would of course prove of great value, but which might well give more systematic and historical treatment than it was within his purpose to attempt. The service which the Ruskin Drawing School, thus re-organized, might render to the cause of artistic education throughout the country is very great. Whether Oxford is ever likely to produce a flourishing School of Art may well be doubted; but there is no reason whatever why it should not set a standard for schools and museums of art elsewhere. What Manchester with inferior resources has recently tried to do,* Oxford has unique means of doing to much greater effect. The hope and endeavour of all those who believe in the humanizing mission of Art is that an Art Gallery—small but select, and simple though complete within its range—should be established in every town, and even in every school. The essential purposes of such collections must be those which Mr. Ruskin had in view in arranging his Drawing School—to exhibit what is best in each department of Art, to

* See an interesting letter from Mr. T. C. Horsfall, Treasurer of the Manchester Art Museum, in the *Times* of November 26th, 1889.

illustrate historical development, to stimulate
or suggest the love of the natural objects pour-
trayed, and to arrange such a course of practical
study as shall incidentally conduce to the previous purposes. Of collections of this kind
Oxford might well set the standard. In each
University generation there are many young
men at Oxford who in after life will have opportunities not only for the patronage of Art in
the sense of private picture-buying, but for the
popularization of Art by bringing it within the
reach of the people. The Ruskin Drawing
School, efficiently arranged and catalogued,
might become a valuable storehouse of suggestions for the utilization of such opportunities.
Every year, too, the University is coming into
closer contact with the provinces, and the number of earnest men and women, eager for the
extension of University teaching in all kinds,
who visit Oxford on the occasion of the "Summer Meetings," is already .very considerable.
To them, too, the Ruskin Drawing School is
capable of being made a source of very useful
inspiration. Moreover; if the collections were
once properly completed, the fame of them
would soon be noised abroad, and any committee

or individual, desirous of doing something to bring Art into schools or villages, would turn to Oxford as the natural quarter for guidance and example. This reorganization of the Ruskin Drawing School would be the best national purpose to which the University could turn the treasures committed to its charge. It would also be the best way of honouring the giver of them. Mr. Ruskin's connection with the School is already commemorated—as well as in its name—by a marble bust of himself, executed by Sir J. E. Boehm.* But the generosity and self-devotion of the founder of the School is surely deserving also of that more acceptable memorial which consists in giving wider fulfilment of his purposes.

---

* See frontispiece. The bust bears the following inscription :—

"Hanc
JOHANNIS RUSKIN
Hujusce scholæ fundatoris
Effigiem
Amici posuerunt
1881."

CHAPTER III.

MR. RUSKIN'S services to National Education have by no means been confined to his work at Oxford. Of his deep interest in the subject, no reader either of " Modern Painters " or of " The Stones of Venice " will need to be reminded. * Some years ago Mr. Ruskin announced it as " probable that a volume especially devoted to the subject of Education may be composed of passages gathered out of the entire series of my works " (Preface to " In Montibus Sanctis "). This probability has not yet become an accomplished fact, perhaps because of the superabundance of material which would await the composer of such a volume.†

* See, especially, " Modern Painters," vol. iv., Appendix 3, and " Stones of Venice," Appendix 7.

† The passages in "Fors Clavigera " "especially devoted to the subject of Education " are enumerated in Mr. Faunthorpe's excellent index. The enumeration occupies nearly seven pages.

In this matter, as in others, Mr. Ruskin has practised what he preached. He has not merely propounded theories on the subject of education, but has never lost an opportunity of putting them into practice. Readers of "Fors Clavigera" and of some others of his later books will recall many allusions to educational experiments made by Mr. Ruskin at the village school of Coniston. What in his old age he does at Brantwood he did long ago in his prime at Denmark Hill. The new Bibliography shows us how indefatigable a lecturer he has been, and most of his minor books were originally composed with direct educational purpose. "The Political Economy of Art" was delivered as lectures at Manchester. "The Elements of Drawing" was a school text-book; and true to the principle explained in the last chapter, that the teaching of Art is the teaching of everything, the text-book contained instructions on what books to read, as well as on what lines to draw. "The Two Paths," "Sesame and Lilies," and "The Crown of Wild Olive" were all written as lectures; whilst "The Ethics of the Dust" was written for a girls' school. But the chief of Mr. Ruskin's earlier educational efforts was in

connection with the Working Men's College.
Of his work there, thirty years ago, and of his
relations with F. D. Maurice, the founder of the
College, some account was given in a recent
chapter of "Præterita" (vol. iii., ch. i.). The
following further reminiscences are supplied by
a friend who himself, too, has done yeoman's
service to the same institution. "The other
day," he says, "I was in the room of an old Art
pupil of Mr. Ruskin's, at the Working Men's
College. Seeing a very clever sketch of a dead
bird, in carmine lake, on the wall, I admired it,
and asked whose it was. 'John Ruskin's,' said
my friend. 'You know he used to come up to
our easels, one after the other, and tell us where
we were right, with a word of praise, and where
wrong, with a "Look here! this is the way to
do that." Well, that bird which you've just
admired Ruskin did one night, on the edge of
my drawing-paper, in less than ten minutes, to
give me a hint. He dashed the sketch in as
fast as brush would go, and the breast, which is
so effective, he did by dabbing the inside of his
thumb on the wet paint. I wouldn't part with
it for anything. A year or two ago he came
to see me, and I showed him his sketch, and

reminded him of when and how he did it. Of course he'd forgotten all about it. But he looked at it, and said, smilingly, " Well, it's very well done." And so it is.' It was in the drawing-room of the Working Men's College," continues the same writer, "that Mr. George Allen, Mr. Ruskin's publisher and engraver, then a working carpenter and joiner, was trained; and no loyaller or better pupil ever lived. There, too, the late Mr. Bunney, whose Venice paintings are so well known, got his teaching and the support of Mr. Ruskin. Mr. William Ward, the skilful copyist of Turner, was another pupil. It is pleasant to hear Mr. Ruskin's old students talk of him; even if they do not agree with his political economy, they do with his art." Another devoted " Ruskinian," whose disciple-ship began at the Working Men's College, was the late Mr. Henry Swan, the first Curator of the St. George's Museum.

Mr. Ruskin's services to the College were not confined to his own work as an Art-teacher. It was at his prompting * that D. G. Rossetti also acted for some years (1857–60) in the

* See Mr. W. M. Rossetti's life of his brother, p. 145, and " Præterita," vol. iii., p. 27.

same capacity.   Amongst those encountered by
Rossetti, at the College, was Mr. Smetham, who
was then a pupil in the drawing-class.   Mr.
Ruskin has spoken two or three times in terms
of disappointment of the work of the College,
but if all its old teachers influenced so many
capable men, and left such pleasant memories
behind them, as did Mr. Ruskin, then the
leaven of Maurice's institution must have gone
very far.

CHAPTER IV.

NEXT to the organization of his Oxford Schools, the most systematic attempt Mr. Ruskin has made to put his educational theories into practice has been in connection with the St. George's Museum, which was expressly intended to illustrate his view of the educational function of the ideal museum. Of this attempt we shall speak in the next chapter. Meanwhile we may pass to notice another educational scheme of Mr. Ruskin's, which has been in actual operation for some years, and has already done much useful service. Much of Mr. Ruskin's work, it is said, is only in the air; but the scheme which we have now to describe is on the solid earth, sweetening with its presence the hard realities of a college in connection with the State. Some ten years ago, the Rev. J. P. Faunthorpe, the Principal of the Whitelands

Training College in Chelsea, chanced to fall
into correspondence with Mr. Ruskin.   He had
noted some passage in "Fors Clavigera," be-
tokening, he thought, undue despondency at
the existing machinery of National Education.
Mr. Ruskin was keenly interested in what Mr.
Faunthorpe had to tell him, and was constant
in counsel and encouragement.   Would Mr.
Ruskin present the College, Mr. Faunthorpe
asked, with a prize?   No; Mr. Ruskin did not
approve of prizes, at least not if there were any
taint of competition about them; but he would
be proud to present the College with a complete set of his works.   The offer was warmly
accepted; and Mr. Ruskin, ever avaricious of
giving, asked to be allowed to present the
College with the means for organizing a "May
Queen" Festival.   In each year he would present the queen with a gold cross for herself,
and with some forty bound volumes, more or
less, of his books for her to award to her fellows
at her will and pleasure.   Mr. Faunthorpe
cheerfully undertook the organization of the
scheme, which was first carried out in 1881,
and has since been continued year by year.
From time to time there have been some slight

I

modifications in the ceremonial. The queen's gown, for one thing, has been altered two or three times. Miss Kate Greenaway designed one, but Mr. Ruskin did not like it; it was a mere robe, he said, and made its wearer look like "Madge Wildfire." The gown for 1889 was designed by Mrs. Faunthorpe. The cross, too, is of different workmanship each year, being designed sometimes by Mr. Burne-Jones, sometimes by Mr. or Mrs. Arthur Severn, sometimes by other artists. One year the cross was composed out of a spray of hawthorn blossom, and Mr. Ruskin complained because there was no thorn, "as if a true queen's crown could ever be without its thorn." But in all essentials the May Queen Festival at White-lands has been the same from year to year; and the following account of the ceremony in 1885, written at the time, may serve as well as another to show the spirit and the scope of this characteristic scheme, designed by the "unpractical" Mr. Ruskin:—

"The celebration of May Day is one of the glories which have pretty well passed away from the earth by this time. The world is too much with us; and as for sports on the merry green, we are too old for that

THE MAY QUEEN'S GOLD CROSS (1888).

(*Designed by Arthur Severn.*)

sort of thing. Indeed, did not Piers say long ago, in
'The Shepherd's Calendar'—

> ' For younkers, Palinode, such follies fitte,
> But we tway bene well of elder witte ' ?

And according to an authority which is always worth
consulting as a sort of 'prosometer,' as a test of how
far the power of prosaic utterance can go, 'the only
people now interested in the maintenance of May sports
are the chimney-sweepers ; for as the commencement
of summer deprives them in a considerable degree
of their business occupation, they naturally seek to
avail themselves of the customary liberality of festive
meetings.'

"But the poetry of May Day still lingers here and
there, even in London. There is Whitelands College,
at Chelsea, for instance, which held high festival yester-
day, and presented a spectacle such as can only be seen
else in Spenser's poems or Miss Greenaway's drawings.
Whitelands is a Training College for Girls, and the
'old girls,'* whose work now lies in country parishes,
do not forget the First of May, but send up large
hampers of spring flowers for decorating the 'dear old
college.' You pass in through the iron gate in the
King's Road, and find yourself in such a company of
sweet flowers as you will not see the like of anywhere
else in the town. Chapel and hall are alike bedecked,
and 'themselves the sweetest flowers among them all'
are the young girls, dressed all of them in their smartest
gowns (there were no bishops present, in lawn sleeves,
to detect the sinful satin shoes), and each wearing
bunches and carrying baskets of flowers. Very pretty

---

* And many of them now, 1891, have a May Queen in their
schools.

it is to see the fresh young faces of the girls, a hundred and fifty, perhaps, or more, gathered thus together in the chapel, 'not taken out of the world in monastic sorrow, but kept from its evil in shepherded peace.' They are possessed now with common interests and common hopes, and the sweet voice that sings, 'Oh, rest in the Lord' is speaking for them all. But there are 'more variations in women's life than any one would imagine from the sameness of women's coiffure ;' and as one's eye lights on the saints in the painted windows one turns to wonder which may be a S. Theresa in the congregation below.

"But it is only after the chapel service is over that the Whitelands peculiar festival begins. It is a festival, held this year for the fifth time, which was instituted and is maintained by Mr. Ruskin, and which realizes in very quaint and pretty fashion many of his 'romantic impossibilities' about education. When the girls are assembled in the hall they are bidden to proceed at once to the business of the day—the election of one among them to be May Queen. There is much sweet excitement, delightful to behold, to know on whom the choice will fall, for the voting is secret (is that, by the way, quite Ruskinian ?) ; and it is only when May Day comes round that the teachers discover who the school favourite is. This year it is a beautiful brunette, but she is chosen not for her beauty nor for learning, but, like the Rosière of Nanterre, simply because in the 'fierce white light' of her schoolfellows she has done her duty and made herself beloved. The election is ratified by much clapping of hands, and the Queen then retires to be robed and crowned. Among her hand-maidens is last year's Queen, the 'Dowager,' now crowned only with forget-me-nots. The girls form in

procession, and when the Queen has taken her place on
the throne, pass, two and two, in front of her, and make
their obeisance.   Mr. Ruskin was not present yester-
day himself, and the gold cross which he gives each
year to the May Queen was presented for him by Mrs.
Bishop.   But a true queen takes more pleasure in
giving than receiving, and it is her turn next to dis-

THE MAY QUEEN'S PROCESSION.

(*From a drawing by Edith Capper.*)

tribute thirty-four volumes of Mr. Ruskin's works, given
by the author, bound in sumptuous purple calf and gold,
to those of her subjects whom she chooses.   There is
no competition about these prizes.   One girl receives
a prize 'because she is faithful to her friends,' another
'because she is fond of music,' another 'for her sunny

temper,' another just 'because the May Queen likes her.' It was particularly pretty to notice the smile of recognition that the Queen—pale and nervous else— would give as some particular friend came up to kiss hands on receiving a prize ; but, indeed, in every way the scene was as pretty as could be, as delicately worked out and as full of suggestion as a sentence in one of Mr. Ruskin's books themselves.

"Mr. Ruskin's festival gives, it is clear, a great deal of innocent pleasure, and certainly they repay him at Whitelands College with their best. His motto, 'To-day,' was placed on their walls ; they prayed for him in their chapel service ; and in the address which Mr. Faunthorpe, the Principal, delivered to the girls yester-day, they were taught to regard him as one of the major prophets, as doing for this age what Plato, Aristotle, and Bacon have done for others. A hundred years hence, Mr. Faunthorpe told them, the nineteenth cen-tury will be remembered only or chiefly because Ruskin lived and wrote in it—which is giving him a victory with a vengeance over his enemies the steam-engines and the railways. However that may be, the girls who go out from Whitelands College to teach throughout the country could take no better friends with them than Mr. Ruskin's books. Those who know most of the deficiencies of our educational curriculum will appreciate best the value to young teachers of so spiritual and stimulating an influence." *

The influence of the May Day Festival at Whitelands soon made itself felt elsewhere.

* *Pall Mall Gazette*, May 2nd, 1885.

The May Queens and other pupils who go out
from Chelsea to be teachers in National schools
carry with them the traditions of the place, and
become themselves centres of similar sweetness
and light.   Not a year passes, Mr. Faunthorpe
tells me, without his hearing of some new May
Day Festival, and in many a country village
wealthy friends have been found to follow
Mr. Ruskin's generous example.   But the most
interesting of these derivative festivals is in
Ireland, where Mr. Ruskin himself again plays
the earthly providence.   One of the Whitelands
governesses, Miss Martin, was appointed a few
years ago to be Head Mistress of the High
School for Girls in Cork, and Mr. Ruskin at
once acceded to her request to establish a similar festival there.   The Queen in this case—for
reasons which readers of " Præterita " will guess
—is a Rose Queen, instead of a Queen of the
May; but Mr. Ruskin presents her in each year
with a gold cross and with a series of his works
for presentation to her chosen Maids of Honour,
at at Whitelands.*   Mr. Ruskin has also presented Miss Martin's school with a case of

* A full and interesting account of the festival appeared
in the *Cork Constitution*, May 2nd, 1888.

rare and costly minerals, stones, and gems.
The case includes specimens of Mocha stone,
agate, jasper, flint, diamonds, gold, silver, mica,
quartz, amethysts, beryls, and other precious
stones.   Some of the specimens are exceedingly rare and exquisitely beautiful.   There
are five uncut Brazilian diamonds, which are
probably worth £40, showing variations of colour
—white, pale yellow, green, and steel grey ; a
really fine nugget of gold in quartz, weighing
about two ounces, and a tress of native silver
with a trace of copper and some other metal.
There are several specimens of amethysts and
quartz, from Brazil, and three from the Ballin-
temple "diamond" quarry, Blackrock.   Mr.
Ruskin has, in addition, presented the school
with eighteen of his original drawings, made
for the illustration of "The Stones of Venice,"
and four of the originals of the plates in the
chapters on Vegetation in "Modern Painters."
He has also given an illuminated cover for an
ancient Persian missal.   The design is in gold
and colours, of conventional flower and leaf
work.   A further gift was a hand-painted ornament, consisting of two panels from the "Book
of Kells."   Accompanying Mr. Ruskin's gift

was the following description of twelve of the
specimens :—

"(1) The best external beginning of Mocha stone I
ever saw, but they may, perhaps, be common at this
locality.   You can find out at leisure.

"(2) Agate, interrupted by quartz veins, which I have
described at greater length somewhere.   It cannot be
too carefully looked at with pocket lens, and may
some day be a classical stone.

"(3) Jasper with green coating.   I believe Scottish,
of quite infinite interest, and infinitely multiplied into
infinite interest.   By the time the youngest pupil in the
school is ninety she may know something about it.

"(4) Banded agate and jasper.   Scotch ; beat it in
Ireland if you can.

"(5) Jasper passing into lake agate, an articular
agate.   Scotch also ; but perhaps you may beat it at
the Giant's Causeway.

"(6) Undulating jasper.   I never thought to part
with it, but it will be better at Cork.

"(7) Common black-handed flint.   A rolled pebble.

"(8) Uncommon handed flint, price 1s. 6d. ; but I
don't think you will get the like of it for 2s. 6d.

"(9) Globulæ mica, the American fashion ; but it
will never make such good mountain as the old-
fashioned mica.

"(10) Straight amianthus in quartz.   Pretty, but the
value of the specimen is in the three unpolished plains,
with endlessly complex and with extremely minute
cavities, looking like spots.

"(11) Five stories of fairy amethyst mountain.   Extremely rare and beautiful.

"(12) The last specimen I have of Sidmouth rock chert, becoming jasper by infusion of colour, reds and yellow oxides of iron. Everywhere a beautiful enigma."

But Mr. Ruskin's interest in Whitelands College, and influence upon the successive generations of its scholars, are not confined to the May Day Festival. He has presented the institution with a cabinet of sixty drawings, and other valuable pictures, books, minerals, and manuscripts, all of which are carefully arranged for use by the girls, and for some of which Mr. Ruskin himself has written descriptive notes. The presence of all these beautiful things in the different rooms of the College lends a very attractive appearance to the place. The walls of the Refectory are covered with interesting pictures and prints, including some copies from Carpaccio, one drawing by Prout, some plates from the "Liber Studiorum," and a series of coloured prints from Bettoni's "Birds of Lombardy," all presented by Mr. Ruskin. In the Governesses' Room there are further gifts of the same kind; whilst the "Ruskin Library" comprises not only many of Mr. Ruskin's own books, but a collection of other books given to the College by him. But the chief Ruskin treasures are in the room of the Principal, where every Sunday evening during term time some of the girls go to examine the books and pictures. Amongst the books is a very fine copy of Bishop Gawin Douglas's "English Virgil"—

"Imprinted at London in 1553,"

to which Mr. Ruskin has added, in printing of his own hand—

"And given
To the College for training of English maids
at Chelsea on Thames,
. by
JOHN RUSKIN,
On the Christmas Day of 1880."

Another very interesting book is an Arabic Koran, in silken satchel with a gold cord, every page being profusely ornamented in flower scrolls and gold. Three large folio volumes, containing water-colour copies made for Mr. Ruskin by hand from Rinio's "Erbario," show the lavish generosity with which he has enriched the College. The Ruskin Cabinet, containing sixty drawings—illustrative of the work of Richter, Dürer, and Turner—framed and mounted in

the same way as the examples in the Ruskin
Drawing School, is of great interest and value.
Mr. Ruskin wrote some notes for his cabinet,
which have been published in the *Ruskin Reading Guild Journal* for 1889. The College,
it is pleasant to know, has met Mr. Ruskin's
generosity in a corresponding spirit. Everything that he has given is well cared for, and
made available for every-day use and influence.
Everywhere, too, throughout the College, the
educational value of beautiful things is recognized and enforced, and not one class-room or
dormitory is without its exemplary picture.
Whitelands is a College where the teachers
of to-morrow are themselves taught, and the
influence for good which Mr. Ruskin's work
there has set on foot throughout the country
must be very great. The Oxford Drawing
School is the practical realization of Mr.
Ruskin's ideal for Schools of Art. Whitelands
College shows in practice the ideal of the movement towards providing "Art for Schools." *

* The address of the "Art of Schools Association" (of
which Mr. Ruskin is the President, and to which his writings gave the initial impetus) is 29, Queen Square, W.C.

CHAPTER V.

(*With some Account of the "Ruskin Museum" at Sheffield.*)

MR. RUSKIN'S experiments as a Social Reformer were, as we have seen (p. 27), a necessary consequence of his Principles of Art. "No great arts are practicable," he says, "by any people, unless they are living contented lives, in pure air, out of the way of unsightly objects, and emancipated from unnecessary mechanical occupation. It is simply one part of the practical work I have to do in Art teaching to bring, somewhere, such conditions into existence, and to show the working of them" ("Fors Clavigera," 1871, ix., p. 20). It was the determination to carry out this duty that led to the formation of the St. George's Guild—the best-known and most-discussed of all Mr. Ruskin's practical works. The ideas underlying the

Guild were, indeed, no new development in his
mind. For many years past he had been ex-
horting "the gentlemen of England" to become,
as he was fond of expressing it, "soldiers of
the ploughshare." But few or none had listened
to his exhortations. "However, this," he said,
"is partly my own fault for not saying more
clearly what I want, and for expecting people
to be moved by writing, instead of by personal
effort. The more I see of writing, the less I
care for it; one may do more with a man by
getting ten words spoken to him face to face
than by the black-lettering of a whole life's
thought" ("Fors," 1872, xvii., p. 5). Giving
up, then, his reliance on mere writing, he set
himself first to talking face to face with such as
had ears to hear—in "Fors Clavigera"—and
secondly to practising what he preached.

It was in May, 1871, that the scheme was first
made public. In the "Fors" for that month
Mr. Ruskin called on any landlords to come and
help him "who would like better to be served
by men than by iron devils," and any tenants and
any workmen who could vow to work and live
faithfully for the sake of the joy of their homes.
Any such as joined St. George's standard were

to do as Mr. Ruskin undertook henceforth to do, and give the tenth of what they had and what they earned, not to emigrate with, but to stay in England with, and make a Happy England of her once more. And this was how the happy days that are no more were to be restored :—

"We will try," said Mr. Ruskin, "to make some small piece of English ground beautiful, peaceful, and fruitful. We will have no steam-engines upon it, and no railroads ; we will have no untended and unthought-of creatures on it ; none wretched, but the sick ; none idle, but the dead. We will have no liberty upon it, but instant obedience to known law and appointed persons ; no equality upon it, but recognition of every betterness that we can find, and reprobation of every worseness. When we want to go anywhere we will go there quietly and safely, not at forty miles an hour, at the risk of our lives ; when we want to carry anything anywhere we will carry it either on the backs of beasts or on our own, or in carts or boats ; we will have plenty of flowers and vegetables in our gardens, plenty of corn and grass in our fields—and few bricks. We will have some music and poetry ; the children shall learn to dance in it and sing in it—perhaps some of the old people, in time, may also. We will have some art, moreover ; we will at least try if, like the Greeks, we can't make some pots. The Greeks used to paint pictures of gods on their pots ; we probably cannot do as much, but we may put some pictures of insects on them, and reptiles—butterflies and frogs, if nothing

better. There was an excellent old potter in France
who used to put frogs and vipers into his dishes, to
the admiration of mankind ; we can surely put something nicer than that. Little by little, some higher art
and imagination may manifest themselves among us,
and feeble rays of science may dawn for us. Botany,
though too dull to dispute the existence of flowers ; and
history, though too simple to question the nativity
of men ; nay, even perhaps an uncalculating and un-
covetous wisdom, as of rude Magi, presenting, at such
nativity, gifts of gold and frankincense."

In taking stock of what Mr. Ruskin has actually done towards realizing this Utopia it is
important to remember the limitations which
he expressly made to his enterprise. He had
no thought of setting himself up as leader in
any large movement. He did not even devote
all his time to the work. On the contrary, he
went into it during the very years when, as
we have already seen, he was busily engaged
at Oxford. His socialistic work was, to use a
current piece of political slang, a payment of
"ransom." He wanted to ease his conscience,
and to feel free once more to devote himself
single-hearted to the arts and sciences. His
object was to quit himself of responsibility by
showing what each man might do. "My march-
ing days " he said, "may perhaps soon be over,

and the best that I can make of myself be a
faithful sign-post. But what I am, or what I
fail to be, is of no moment to the cause. The
two facts which I have to teach, or sign, though
alone, as it seems, at present, in the signature,
that food can only be got out of the ground, and
happiness only out of honesty, are not altogether dependent on any one's championship,
for recognition among mankind" (" Fors,"
1873, xxx., p. 19).

" That food can only be got out of the ground,
and happiness out of honesty." These were
the first two facts which the Guild of St. George
was established to demonstrate; and the third
was the fact (to cite once more Prince Leopold's
felicitous words) that " the highest wisdom and
the highest treasure need not be costly or
exclusive" (see p. 45, *n.*). The enforcement of
these three facts leads us, it will be seen, to
three corresponding experiments, of (1) an
agricultural, (2) an industrial, and (3) an artistic character, respectively. The first and the
second cannot, indeed, be very trenchantly distinguished; but it will be more convenient to
treat separately the distinctively industrial part
of " St. George's " scheme: that will form the

K

subject of the next chapter. In the present
chapter we must notice briefly Mr. Ruskin's
experiments under the other two heads.

The agricultural experiments of the St.
George's Guild have not been a brilliant success. Perhaps they have not been given a fair
chance. Perhaps the times and seasons have
been unpropitious. But whatever explanations
or excuses there may be, the fact remains that
the St. George's farms have produced very
little except a plentiful crop of disappointments.
Mr. Ruskin has drawn many charming pictures,
such as the one given above, of his ideal settlements; but the realities have for the most part
been either grim or grotesque, or (more often)
both. The Guild is, however, the owner of
several acres of land in different parts of the
country, and there is some reason to hope that
past failures will lead to future successes. If
there are any disciples of Count Tolstoi who,
having decided "what to do," are casting about
for plots of ground on which to do it, they
should communicate with the Trustees of St.
George's Guild.*

* Particulars of some of the agricultural experiments
referred to above will be found in many places throughout

EXTERIOR OF THE ST. GEORGE'S MUSEUM, WALKLEY.

Meanwhile it is pleasant to turn to a branch of St. George's work which, within its appointed range, has been completely successful already, and which is now destined to be more widely useful. This is the St. George's Museum, hitherto housed in a cottage at Walkley, situated upon a hill two miles out of Sheffield. It was intended to be not a show place, but rather a model of the Museum which might profitably and practically be established in every town, and the lowly aspect of the building at Walkley is in keeping with the modest object of the institution. Mr. Ruskin has himself explained why he selected Sheffield to be the site of his experiment :—

"The answer is a simple one—That I acknowledge iron-work as an art necessary and useful to man, and English work in iron as masterful of its kind. . . . Therefore it is fitting that of the schools (of St. George) for the workmen and labourers of England, the first should be placed at Sheffield. Besides this merely systematic and poetical fitness, there is the further practical reason for our first action being among this

"Fors." The "Master's Reports" contain further information. Mr. Ruskin's "General Statement, explaining the Nature and Purposes of St. George's Guild," may be obtained from Mr. George Allen (6d.).

order of craftsmen in England, that in cutler's iron-work
we have (in the town of Sheffield) at this actual epoch
of our history the best of its kind done by English hands,
unsurpassable, I presume, when the workman chooses
to do all he knows, by that of any living nation ; not
for this reason only, however, but because Sheffield is
in Yorkshire, and Yorkshire is yet in the main temper
of its inhabitants Old English, and capable, therefore,
yet of the ideas of honesty and piety by which Old
England lived ; finally, because Sheffield is within easy
reach of beautiful natural scenery, and the best art of
English hands, at Lincoln, York, Durham, Selby, Foun-
tains, Bolton, and Furness. For these great primary
reasons, including many others, I have placed our first
Museum there, in good hope also that other towns, far
and near, when they see how easily such a thing can
be done, will have their museums of the same kind, as
no less useful to them than their churches, gasometers,
or circulating libraries."

Sheffield, it may be added, has justified Mr.
Ruskin's choice by meeting his generosity in
an admirably practical fashion, as we shall presently see.

As for the contents of the Museum in general,
the following description is given in the Catalogue prepared by Mr. Howard Swan, son of
the late Curator :—

"The Museum contains specimens, copies, casts, etc.,
selected by John Ruskin, of the truly greatest of human
art of the times of the highest development in each

INTERIOR OF ST. GEORGE'S MUSEUM, WALKLEY.

branch, and from those parts of the world where they best flourished, so arranged and explained as to be—first, a readily accessible repository of specimens of the finest work hitherto done, whether in painting, illumination, engraving, drawing, or sculpture, etc., and of the finest natural productions, in the shape of crystalized gems and precious stones ; it will have nothing in it but what deserves respect in art or admiration in nature ; secondly, a guide to the rise and development of nations, as evidenced in their art ; thirdly, a school of drawing and painting, with examples and instructions, after the manner of the old Tuscan masters, as set forth in Mr. Ruskin's 'The Laws of Fésole,' in which things interesting in natural history or in legend are utilized as drawing copies, while a true system of training the eye and hand is taught."

The reader who wishes for more detailed information about the contents will find all he wants in the Catalogue just cited.*   For the purposes of a desultory look round, we cannot do better than put ourselves in Mr. Ruskin's hands.   In 1879 the late Prince Leopold spent some time at the Museum, and Mr. Ruskin pointed out to him the chief objects of interest. From the account of this visit published in the *Sheffield Independent* I borrow the following particulars.   Mr. Ruskin first drew attention

* It may be obtained of Mr. George Allen, price 1*s*.

to Verocchio's " Madonna and Child," the only
specimen of that master in this country,* and
"given to me," added Mr. Ruskin, "in Venice
by a gracious fortune, to show to the people
of Sheffield," to whom, he explained, it was
especially appropriate, since, besides being an
unrivalled painter, Verocchio was also a great
worker in iron. Mr. Ruskin dwelt with enthusiasm on the teachings and technical merits of
this picture—on its lessons of the reverence
that is due to woman, and the reverence that
all Christianity, through that, its purest element,
shows (in the kneeling Virgin) to Christ. That
picture, he said, was an answer to the inquiry
often addressed to him, "What do you want
to teach us about Art?" It was perfect in
all ways—in drawing, in colouring; on every
part the artist had worked with the utmost toil
man could give. He drew especial attention to
the beauty and detail of the Virgin's girdle of
embossed gold. A copy, by Mr. Ruskin, of

* I do not know the genealogy of Mr. Ruskin's Verocchio.
But in the National Gallery there are two pictures (296
and 781) ascribed either to Verocchio or to Pollajuolo. See
" Popular Handbook to the National Gallery " (Macmillan),
under 296 (in Room I.).

Carpaccio's "St. Ursula" next attracted attention. The power of that Museum would, Mr.
Ruskin went on to say, depend upon its giving
pleasure, and by the attractions of beauty, but
as the foundation from which all teaching must
start, they had there the most perfect specimens of the Bible—the Baskerville, the German
Zurich Bible, with plates mostly by Holbein
and Dürer—which are unequalled for perfect
illustration of the meaning of the Scriptures.
Then there were elaborate specimens of English
illuminated MSS. of the Vulgate, and following
these the first perfect copy of Holbein's "Dance
of Death." After that again came Carpaccio's
"Death of St. Jerome," the translator of the
Bible into Latin; and then St. George.

Turning from these illustrative keys to the
teachings of his Museum, Mr. Ruskin drew
his visitor's attention to his unique collection of minerals and precious stones—to the
specimens of gold and virgin silver, amethyst,
onyx stone, and many other unrivalled examples
of the wonders of mineralogy. "I want," said
he, "to get everything beautiful;" and in answer to a question, he added, "I am proud to
say that, unlike other collectors, I never spare

cutting my specimens, always looking to that
which will best show texture. My main aim
is to get things to show their beauty." Then
passing from the upper case of precious stones
and minerals, Mr. Ruskin showed many of the
treasures in the drawers, beginning with the
simple flint pebble, and passing on in natural
succession to jasper and agates, to specimens
of which, showing all the wondrous laws of
their structure, he called attention; then on
to quartz and felspar; "and so we get," said
he, "the constituents of granite; and getting
that, you go on to the constituents of everything
else." Then there were amethysts, cut so as to
show their stellar form, and opals and crystals,
with their perfectly natural facets—types of a
beauty with which it is Mr. Ruskin's hope to
attract working men to an interest in the structure of such things.

Turning next to the cabinets, in which are
stored his etchings and photographs, Mr. Ruskin showed a photograph from that earliest
church in Venice on which is inscribed his
favourite legend, enjoining on the merchants to
be just, and to have their weights true. That,
said Mr. Ruskin, was the beginning of the whole

commercial prosperity of Venice; from that came
the pure gold of the Venetian *zecchini* (ducats).
Mr. Firth would, he thought, be interested to
know that when he was daguerreotyping in
Venice, and wanted absolutely pure gold for his
plates, he could get nothing so pure as these
old Venetian coins; and all the city's prosperity
was the outcome of that honest thoroughness.
A series of photographs from Venice, showing
the various forms of the Greek acanthus, was
exhibited, Mr. Ruskin drawing especial attention to the variety introduced by the play of
the workman's hand, no one leaf being like another. In drawings of his own which he produced, Mr. Ruskin said his object had been to
show how our English leaves were adapted to
the same treatment—the oak leaf, for instance.
He hoped to show a series of rude carvings by
Sheffield boys and girls, from natural leaves.
He was going to have a series carved in wood,
and the cabbage or kale would be the first, for
that was the vegetable which in the North was
the origin of our most beautiful sculptures. Mr.
Ruskin showed with pride a cast of one of the
vine leaves from the Ducal Palace, displaying
admirably, with a fidelity that nothing could

rival, the patient skill of the workman of the
fourteenth century, and an edge than which
nothing could be finer or clearer.

Next Mr. Ruskin drew attention to a rough
block of sandstone—a specimen showing the
pure cleavage of the sands of England, "which,
thanks again to 'Fors,' I was able to take from
Brantwood." The lesson herein was characteristic of the whole teaching of the Museum—a
leading up from the simplest thing to those
greater things on which he had been discours-
ing; and turning to the Prince, Mr. Ruskin
observed, "You, sir, said in your most excellent address that England is the mother of great
nations. May we not teach her to remember
also that she has great ancestors?" With reference to his projects in regard to the Museum,
Mr. Ruskin said he did not want to build another room until he got that one room into
perfect condition. Then, when that room was
made the vestibule, and in this way showing the
source of all beauty, as he got power—having
been quietly acquiring the necessary land—he
hoped to make reading-rooms for the workmen, which they could use in connection with
this room. Drawing his Royal Highness's

attention to the beautiful view from the windows, now lighted up by gleams of sunlight, Mr. Ruskin continued, "I hope always to have pretty things for them to see, and light to read by, and fitting everything close as I do so. And I hope it may be filled by workmen who will join to scientific teaching this study of art and nature, and that it will be felt by the town worth making an effort to fill the rooms with books." "If anything now fails," added Mr. Ruskin, modestly, "it will be my fault ' but he was understood to say that the town authorities would find him in every way obedient to their desires—as his Royal Highness would do him the justice of admitting that he was ever submissive to the powers of the land, as represented by her most Gracious Majesty and her royal children.

A king's treasury such as this which was disclosed to the Prince is worth walking a mile or two, Mr. Ruskin thought, to see, and hence it was that the Museum was set some little way out of the town, perched on a hill, and in the midst of green fields.* For the peculiarity of

* An illustrated article on the Walkley Museum, with some particulars supplied by Mr. Swan, appeared in the

Sheffield among manufacturing towns is the close proximity to it of some of the most beautiful scenery in England. From the front door of the Walkley Museum to the right is an extensive view of the Valley of the Don, with the woods of Wharncliffe Crags far away in the distance; while to the left, and also to be seen from the Museum windows, is that Rivelian valley which Elliot, the Corn-law rhymer, made his favourite resort:—

"Oh that I were a primrose,
    To bask in sunny air,
Far away from the plagues that make
    Town-dwelling men's despair !
Or like a rainbow laughing
    O'er Rivelin and Don,
When misty morning calleth up
    Her mountains one by one."

In the visitors' book it is interesting to note the places from which pilgrims have come— London, Leeds, Hull, Manchester, Chester, Birmingham, Canada, New York, Australia, and

Pall Mall Gazette, May 14th, 1886. From that article I have borrowed the following few paragraphs. Some reminiscences of the late Mr. Swan, "the faithful steward of the Ruskin Museum," appeared in the *Pall Mall Gazette*, April 2nd and 3rd, 1889.

even China. Some of these pilgrims have lodged
in neighbouring cottages, and visited the Museum day after day for as long as six weeks
together. The secret of the attractiveness of
Mr. Ruskin's Museum is its adherence to two
golden rules, which are too often ignored in
more imposing institutions. In the first place,
there is no confusing mass of heterogeneous objects. In quantity there is very little, and everything is co-ordinated in an intelligible scheme
of artistic education. And in the second place,
whatever there is, is beautiful and good of its
kind. The result is, Mr. Ruskin assures us,
that every visitor, of whatever class, to the little
Walkley Museum, who has any real love for
Art, has acknowledged the interest and value
of the things collected in its single room.

The Corporation of Sheffield have throughout shown the warmest interest in the Museum
which Mr. Ruskin thus located near their town.*
Some time ago they proposed to build a grand
new casket for these art treasures, and the
negotiations with Mr. Ruskin were nearly

* The following paragraphs are mostly borrowed from
an article on the Meersbrook Park, by " F.," in the *Pall Mall
Gazette*, January 6th, 1890.

successfully carried through, until the Corporation made it a condition that the treasures should be secured to the town in perpetuity, whereupon Mr. Ruskin waxed wroth, and took to drawing *Anagallis tenella* (or was it wild strawberry ?), and would have no more to do with Mayor or Corporation. But that was long ago, and since then the Guild has fallen on evil days; its honoured Master has been stricken with illness; its farms have gone the way of most farms; but through good report and evil report the faithful Corporation has ever been ready to help the afflicted Guild. At last it became evident that the present building could no longer be tolerated. Every year hundreds of pilgrims were "symbolically instructed" by struggling up that awful hill, and the complaints were loud and many; besides, Walkley could not hold half the treasures. Mr. Baker (one of the trustees) had piles of drawings at Bewdley, many were still at Brantwood, and at Sheffield itself the town clerk's office was idealized by quantities of pictures and minerals, poured out unexpectedly one day at the feet of the Corporation by the all-generous Master. The public had an opportunity a few years ago of seeing

at the Fine Art Society's galleries several specimens of the drawings which Mr. Ruskin had
in recent years commissioned on behalf of the
St. George's Guild.*

But there was no room for them in the Museum. Indeed, already it had been found necessary to put up a wooden shed in the garden,
in order to accommodate the large picture of
the façade of St. Mark's which Mr. Ruskin had
bought from the late Mr. Bunney. Now, by
happy chance Sheffield has lately bought a park
just on the outskirts of the town, and in it
stands a fine old Georgian mansion. In every
way it seems suitable for the Ruskin Museum.
Tram-cars run from the heart of the town to
the edge of the park, then a pleasant walk of
three minutes, up an avenue of old trees, brings
the student to Meersbrook Park. The rooms
are spacious, well-proportioned, and admirably
lighted. There is a long gallery, with three
large windows, and a smaller one excellently
adapted for lectures and classes. Then there
are quiet, airy rooms where students can copy
drawings or study missals, and upstairs is a

* May, 1886. A catalogue of this exhibition, with a pre-
fatory note by Mr. Ruskin, was published.

complete set of living rooms for the curator. All is solid, dry, quiet, and well removed from smoke and dirt. Close to the hall is its fine old garden, enclosed in red brick walls, and 'stocked with an abundance of flowers, fruit, and vegetables.

Nor were these the only features which seemed to mark out Meersbrook Park as the ideal home for the Museum of the St. George's Guild. Did not the Master write hopefully of a "cloistral inn," holy tavern, or other ideal hostelry which (with a no less ideal hostess) was to form part of the Museum? Here, then, is the hope realized, for at the end of a little woodland path is a beautiful open-timbered house, dating back to the early part of the fifteenth century. Two bishops were born there, and the old building is known still as the Bishop's House. I do not presume to judge of the requirements of a cloistral inn, but the old house seems well fitted to comfortably lodge students and visitors. This time the negotiations have been brought to a triumphant ending. The Corporation offered the hall, garden, and Bishop's House to the Guild, conditionally on the art collection being secured to them for twenty years, and the trustees

INTERIOR OF THE PICTURE-GALLERY, MEERSBROOK HALL.

joyfully accepted the offer (August, 1889). It
is a rule of the Guild "that the Master must
not be bothered," so the matter was briefly laid
before Mr. Ruskin, and his cousin, Mrs. Severn,
promptly forwarded his ratification of the scheme.
The mansion has been suitably decorated; the
collections have been transferred to it, and the
new Museum was opened by the Earl of Carlisle
on April 15th, 1890. A greatly enlarged career
of usefulness has thus been opened up for the
Ruskin Museum, which will long remain, we
may hope, as a monument of the Acts promoted
by Mr. Ruskin's "Gospel." *

* The Curator of the Museum is Mr. William White,
from whom all particulars with regard to its rules, hours of
opening, etc., may be obtained.

L

CHAPTER VI.

THE place occupied in Mr. Ruskin's schemes of
practical endeavour by the industrial experiments of the St. George's Guild cannot be better
described than in Mr. Ruskin's own words.
"The notices which I see," he wrote in January,
1886, "in the leading journals, of efforts now
making for the establishment of industrial villages, induce me to place before the members
of the St. George's Guild the reasons for their
association, in a form which may usefully be
commended to the attention of the general public.
The St. George's Guild was instituted with a
view of showing, in practice, the rational organization of country life, independent of that of
cities. All the efforts, whether of the Government
or the landed proprietors of England, for the help
or instruction of our rural population, have been
made under two false suppositions: the first,

that country life was henceforward to be subordinate to that of towns ; the second, that the
landlord was, for a great part of the year, to
live in the town, and thence to direct the management of his estate. Whatever may be the
destiny of London, or Paris, or Rome in the
future, I have always taught that the problem
of right organization of country life was wholly
independent of them ; and that the interests of
the rural population, now thought, by the extension of Parliamentary suffrage, to be placed in
their own keeping, had always been so, and to
the same degree, if they had only known it.
Throughout my writings on social questions I
have pointed to the former life of the Swiss (represented with photographic truth by Jeremías
Gotthelf),* and to the still existing life of the
Norwegians and Tyrolese, perfectly well known
to every thoughtful and kind-hearted traveller in
their respective countries,—as examples, nearly
perfect, of social order independent of cities :—
but with Carlyle, I have taught also that in the
English, French, and Italian natures there was,
superadded to the elements of the German and

* See, *e.g.*, his " Ulric the Farm-servant," translated by
Mrs. Firth (G. Allen).

Norwegian mind, a spirit of reverence for their leaders in worldly things, and for their monitors in spiritual things, which was their greatest strength and greatest happiness, in the forfeiture of which, by their nobles, had passed away their own honour, and on the loss of which, by the people, had followed inevitably the degradation of their characters, the destruction of their arts, and the ruin of their fortunes" ("Master's Report," 1885, pp. 1, 2). The object, then, of the efforts described in this chapter has been to re-create these lost arts, not by organizing "industrial villages," but, what is a very different thing, by reviving village industries.

"A subject which is of the deepest interest to me," wrote Mr. Ruskin, in an earlier report than the one just cited, "is the success of Mr. Albert Fleming in bringing back the old industry of the spinning-wheel to the homes of Westmoreland, greatly increasing their happiness, and effectively their means of support, by the sale, already widely increasing, of the soundest and fairest linen fabrics that care can weave or field-dew blanch." The description of this revived spinning industry given in the first of the following sections has been kindly written for me by Mr. Fleming. "For full account of the kindly and honest trade in homespun work I may," wrote Mr. Ruskin, "happily and thankfully refer the reader to the article in the *Pall Mall Gazette* of Monday, February 8th [1886]. . . . I have nothing more closely at heart, nor can any of my friends oblige me more than by their support of it." The description of this second village industry given in the second section is reprinted from the article referred to by Mr. Ruskin; whilst in the third section I have given some account of an allied experiment in the case of a town industry.

§ I.

THE LANGDALE LINEN INDUSTRY.

[By Mr. Albert Fleming.]

Amongst the evils resulting from the gradual depopulation of the villages is that round us here, in Westmoreland, all the old trades are dying or dead—bobbin-turning, charcoal-burning, woodcarving, basket-making, hand-spinning and weaving—some are clean vanished, and others are the mere ghosts of their old selves. My own personal experiment has been to try and reintroduce the hand-spinning and weaving of linen. For years past Mr. Ruskin has been eloquently beseeching English men and maidens once more to spin and weave. Wordsworth, too, melodiously lamented the disuse of the spinning-wheel; but for all that, it was as practically extinct all over England as our great-grandmothers' sedan chairs. It figured on Covent Garden stage every season, but Margaret's thread was scarcely of a marketable quality. And if the wheels were obsolete, much more so were the distaff and spindle. When Lady Freake's pretty young ladies gave their Greek play some years ago, not one of them (nor the learned Professor who arranged them either) had any idea how to hold her distaff, much less how to spin a thread.

In the face of all this prevailing ignorance I determined to try and bring the art back to the Westmoreland women. Scattered about on the fell side were many old women, too blind to sew and too old for hard work, but able to sit by the fireside and spin, if any one would show them how, and buy their yarn. When I broached my scheme to a circle of practical relations a Babel of expostulation arose, wild as a

Parsifal chorus. "It won't pay; no one wants linen to last fifty years; it's fantastic, impracticable, sentimental, and quixotic." But to balance

PEASANT-WOMAN SPINNING.
(*From a drawing by Edith Capper.*)

all this came a voice from Brantwood, saying, "Go ahead;" so I went ahead, hunted up an old woman who had spun half a century ago, and discovered some wheels of a similar period.

I got myself taught spinning, and then set to work to teach others. I tried my experiment here, in the Langdale Valley, in Westmoreland, half-way between Mr. Ruskin's home at Coniston and Wordsworth's at Rydal. Sixty years ago every cottage here had its wheel, and every larger village its weaver. Happy days those, "before the present years were sought out, or ever the inventions of them that now sin were turned." Our first difficulty was to get wheels; we ransacked the country side, advertised far and wide, and bought and begged anything that had a leg to stand on or a wheel to turn. Delightful old ladies routed out their lumber-rooms and garrets, and here and there a farmer's wife brought tidings of a wheel having been heard of in some remote valley. Some came from Stornoway, and others from the Isle of Man. By-and-by the demand became so great that we held a solemn council with the village carpenter, and ultimately he made us fifteen good serviceable wheels.

What dire difficulties arose over our first home-made wheel! Birmingham either could not or would not turn out the iron fittings, and actually all Sheffield could not make us the

necessary left-handed screws. When that first
wheel was completed and worked well I was

"ST. MARTIN'S," LANGDALE.
(*From a drawing by Edith Capper.*)

ready to bear it in triumph through the streets
like Cimabue's picture. I wanted to carry out

the whole process, from the flax in the field to the sheet on the bed, but that I found impossible, and I have to get my flax from Ireland. Then I took a little cottage, and made it into a spinning school; a quaint place, exactly fulfilling Horace's injunction, "Near the house let there be a spring of water, and a little wood close by." Kind lady friends rallied round me, and gave me practical help in organizing and carrying on the scheme. We soon had many pupils, and applications for wheels came from all sides. When a woman could spin a good thread I let her take a wheel home, and gave her the flax, buying it back from her when spun, at the rate of 2s. 6d. per pound of thread. Next came the weaving. In a cellar in Kendal we discovered a loom; it was in twenty pieces, and when we got it home not all the collective wisdom of the village knew how to set it up. Luckily we had a photograph of Giotto's Campanile, and by help of that the various parts were rightly put together. We then secured an old weaver, and one bright Easter morning saw our first piece of linen woven—the first purely hand-spun and hand-woven linen produced in all broad England in our generation. A significant fact that, if you think all round it.

Over that first twenty yards the scoffers rejoiced greatly.   I own it seemed terrible stuff, frightful in colour and of dreadful roughness, with huge lumps and knots meandering up and down its surface.   But we took heart of grace, and refreshed ourselves by reading that beautiful passage in the " Seven Lamps " (" The Lamp of Life," p. 21) which convinced us that these little irregularities were really the honourable badges of all true hand work.   Better still, an elect lady called one day, and even without the preliminary refreshment of the passage from the " Seven Lamps," she pronounced the stuff delightful, and bought a dozen yards, at four shillings a yard.

Having got our linen, the next process was to bleach it.   I read various treatises on bleaching, and discovered that all the processes were more or less injurious both to workmen and to stuff; so, as Giotto fixed our loom for us, Homer taught us the true principle of bleaching, and we adopted the simple method described in the " Odyssey."   Sun, air, and dew were our only chemicals : potent magicians they, changing by their sweet alchemy our coarse brown stuff into soft white linen.   Now, Mr. Howells puts this

wise axiom into the lips of one of his heroines,
" Before you learn to do a thing, be sure people
want it." To my great delight, I found people

"OLD JOHN," THE WEAVER.
(*From a drawing by Edith Capper.*)

did want real hand-made linen, linen that they
could hand down as family heirlooms, and that
rust and moth could not corrupt. Orders and

inquiries came from all parts of England. Fashion helped us, too, for our linen was eagerly sought after for embroidery, for curtains, portières, chair-backs, tea-cloths, and a dozen other elegant inutilities; so then, to quote the "Spectator," "I took the laudable mystery of embroidery into my serious consideration," and enrolled a staff of about forty poor ladies, who are experienced workers, and for whose work we have a ready sale.

And now to wind up with a few facts. We have two looms going, and about thirty women at work. The old weaver gets a fixed wage of 16s. a week and a good cottage rent free. The best of our spinners earn about 6s. a week. We make seventeen different kinds of linen, varying in price from 2s. to 6s. a yard. The widest linen is 44 inches, and its price is 5s. 6d. a yard. Stout, durable sheeting (very white and soft) is our staple production, but we aspire to table-cloths and body linen by-and-by. All money produced by the sale of linen is paid into the bank, and the profits will be divided among the workers at the end of the year. If any nice old-fashioned people want any of our linen, or care to know anything more

about our little enterprise, let them write to me,
at Neaum Crag, Langdale, Ambleside.

§ 2.

"ST. GEORGE'S" CLOTH.

Some ten years ago, when " Fors Clavigera "
was still running its course, and Mr. Ruskin
was telling all true English girls that among
other things they must learn to spin and weave,
a correspondent wrote to him from Laxey, in
the Isle of Man, to say that there was still a
good deal of spinning done on that little island.
Unfortunately, however, there were no longer
any young girls learning to spin, and there
seemed every prospect that in a few years more
the spinning-wheel would be as great a curiosity
in the Isle of Man as it was already in Lanca-
shire.   The reason was simple enough.   There
was still a healthy native industry for women
in spinning the wool of the Isle-bred sheep, but
the market was so poor that frequently infirm
and aged women were obliged to leave their
cottages and their spinning-wheels to work in
the mines. This was the natural tendency,
everybody said, of inevitable laws; but Mr.

Ruskin was well accustomed to stand *contra mundum*, and determined to make a last effort to save "the venerable art" that was being so remorselessly "torn from the poor."

He at once found his man in the correspondent above referred to, Mr. Egbert Rydings, with whose intelligent help the decrepit industry was quickly put on its legs. Mr. Rydings's heart was in the business : there could be no doubt of that. Why, every blanket and sheet, every piece of flannel and cloth, every pair of stockings, in his house, had been spun either by his wife or by her mother before her. "We have now linen sheets to wear," wrote Mr. Rydings, with pleasant pride, "not a hole or a tear in them, that were spun by my wife's mother—and she, poor body, has been dead twenty-eight or twenty-nine years—the flax grown on their own farm." What do you think of that ? And did not the daughters of Lord Auckland, when he was Bishop of Sodor and Man, go every Saturday afternoon to the dear old lady to learn to spin ? Mr. Rydings was thus reviving a family tradition as well as a village industry. First of all, Mr. Ruskin found money to encourage some of the older and

feebler workers, and he then had a water-mill
built. He has often been accused of prefer-
ring the beautiful to the useful, and I give the
accompanying sketch of St. George's Mill, at
Laxey, to refute the accusation. The author
of "The Seven Lamps of Architecture" and of
"The Stones of Venice" is justifiably proud of
this substantial building, and the photograph
of it, with the accompanying legend, from which
this sketch is taken, occupies a prominent place
among the other art treasures in the drawing-
room at Brantwood. The first virtue in any
building is that it should be suitable to its
purpose, and no one can deny to the Laxey
Mill an honest ugliness which exactly suits the
home "of the manufacture of honest thread
into honest cloth."

This romantic building is at once a factory
and a store. It contains, in the first place, the
machinery for carding and spinning the wool
and washing the cloth. The word machinery
may very probably grate on the ear of the more
devout Ruskinian, and I hasten therefore to
explain that the motive power is a water-wheel.
And it may here be noted, for the consolation
of weaker brethren, that the prohibition of

First achievement] The St George's Company in
Romantic architecture . . J.R. 10th July, 1881.

machinery by "St. George" is not absolute.
It is not forbidden except where it supersedes
healthy bodily exercise or the art and precision
of manual labour. It is only steam that is absolutely refused, as being "a cruel and furious
waste of fuel, to do what every stream and
breeze are ready to do costlessly." The moored
river-mill alone, says Mr. Ruskin, "invented by
Belisarius fourteen hundred years ago, would
do all the mechanical work ever required by a
nation which either possessed its senses or could
use its hands." But Mr. Ruskin's mill is a
store as well, and in this capacity it enables
him to revive another piece of the olden time.
There is a sale in the ordinary way for the outside world, but there is the good old institution
of barter also. The farmers bring their wool,
which is stored in the mill, and are paid for it
either by finished cloth or by yarn for home
knitting, or occasionally by wool prepared for
home spinning. One does not like to think
what the rigid economists would say to this
calculated interference with the division of
labour; but then, as the lives of the peasants
are the healthier, perhaps the other kind of
wealth may be left to look after itself.

M

But in addition to this work of preparing yarn and wool, the "hands" at the mill make a good deal of cloth for outside sale. This, indeed, was an essential part of Mr. Ruskin's scheme. There was no good, he saw, in denouncing people for wearing shoddy unless he could also put them in the way of buying honest cloth. The square yard of Laxey homespun was to be "one of the standards of value in St. George's currency," but it was also to be a standard of material in dress. It is "all wool," for one thing; and for another, it is dyed indelibly, being, indeed, the natural colour of the black sheep of the island, blended in certain proportions of white wool. Anybody who likes cloth warranted not to change colour or to shrink cannot do better (especially just now, when greys are so fashionable) than order a dress length of the Laxey homespun. The Duchess of Albany wrote to Mr. Ruskin a year or two ago, expressing her great pleasure at receiving a length of cloth made by the Guild, in whose work her husband took so great an interest. ·One fault— for I must not conceal its dark side—one fault St. George's cloth cheerfully confesses. It lasts a very long time, and that, Mr. Rydings says, was what made the Manx-made stuffs go out of request : they did not give young women a chance of having four or five new gowns in the year.

But if there are any English housewives ready to forgive this fault, they cannot do better than send some orders to Mr. Rydings (Laxey, Isle of Man), or to Mr. George Thomson (Woodhouse Hill, Huddersfield), who has latterly relieved Mr. Ruskin of the management of the St. George's Mill.

§ 3.

"GEORGE THOMSON AND CO."

The "work according to Ruskin" which has now to be described is not, like the schemes already noticed, directly connected with the St. George's Guild. The prime mover in the matter is, however, one of the trustees of the Guild, and the impetus which launched the scheme five years ago was derived from Mr. Ruskin's teaching. The scheme itself, which is of a more far-reaching kind than the others, is of deep interest in days when the condition of England question is once more in every one's mouth.

Mr. Ruskin is no equalizer. " The division
of property," he has said, " is its destruction ;
and with it the destruction of all hope, all industry, and all justice." But while he does not
wish for any forcible division of property, he has
proposed an almost equally revolutionary scheme
in saying that property should be only "to whom
proper." The capitalist, for instance, has no
right, according to him, to exact interest. Em-
ployers should be paid just wages for their
superintendence of labour, but not for their
capital; that is the sum and substance of Mr.
Ruskin's teaching on the capital and labour
question.

It is this " law of political economy " that one
of the companions and trustees of St. George's
Guild is now carrying out into practice, as far
as he can, in the case of his own business—the
well-known woollen and worsted manufactory
of William Thomson and Sons, at Huddersfield.
Mr. George Thomson, the head of the firm, has
converted it into a productive association on
a truly co-operative basis. The new association
takes over the business at a price, of course ;
but the disposition in which " St. George" makes
bargains of the kind is not quite the same as

that of some other promoters of companies. The amount to be paid was fixed on an independent valuation, and Mr. Thomson decided that such valuation should not include any consideration whatever for goodwill. Further, the whole of the sum, so far as it is not taken up in shares, will be paid for by loan stock, bearing interest at the rate of £5 per cent. per annum, and so long as this interest is paid the principal cannot be demanded; subject to the payment of £5 per cent. on the shares—which in time will largely pass, it may be hoped, into the hands of the workmen and women—half the net profits of the concern will go to the workers. A sum of £500 has already either been earned as profit or deposited as share-capital, by the workers, thus showing their appreciation of the scheme. The moral effect of it on the general character of the workers, in increasing their self-respect and interest in their work, has been particularly noticed by all visitors.

Out of the other half of the profits, equitable allowances are made to customers. The customers so far have been mainly co-operative societies, and 50 per cent. of the net profits is divided amongst all such societies as have done business to the extent of £50 per annum (with net cash payment). The co-operative societies are thus practically their own producers, without the trouble of production. One society received about £20 last year in this way, over and above all that they would have had in the ordinary course of trade.

By this means it is hoped to counteract the constant efforts of buyers to run down articles for buying, and run them up for selling. Mr. Thomson himself—who, by the way, is examiner of cloth manufacture for the City and Guilds of London Technical Institute—remains at the head of the business as manager, and is paid his wages like every one else, sharing in proportion with the other workers, but no more, in such net profits as he may assist in earning. It is a commonplace with capitalists to say that "the interests of capital and labour are identical;" so, no doubt, in a sense they are, even under our existing economical conditions. The same good times, that is to say, that secure to the worker his weekly dole secure to the capitalist his lion's share. But it is only under such co-operative organization as I am describing that the interests of capital and labour are identical in the sense that the capitalist is made a labourer and the labourers are made capitalists.

What Mr. Ruskin himself thinks of the scheme is sufficiently shown in the following letter, which he addressed to Mr. Thomson on the subject in 1886 :—

"I cannot enough thank you, or express the depth of my pleasure in the announcement of the momentous and absolutely foundational step taken by you in all that is just and wise, in the establishment of these relations with your workmen. I may perhaps yet live to see 'the pleasure of the Lord prosper in your hand ;' for though making no sign, I have been steadily advancing in strength, hope, and lately even in youthful enjoyment of former work, and continuance of it on the old terms. 'Præterita' is advancing fast toward the part in which I shall resume the courses of thought which led to writing 'Unto This Last,' and shall throw what I was able to say confusedly into more intelligible and open form. But without your practical power and faith nothing could have been yet done."

This latest development of Mr. Ruskin's political economy is not, of course, a new thing ; but the concern starts under conditions of success and upon genuinely co-operative terms, which have not always attended similar undertakings. It is not an amateur affair, set on foot by philan-

thropic outsiders; it is the result of the appeal
which has for so long been addressed to the
manufacturers themselves to organize their industry on a sounder basis than that of individual
competition. As such Mr. Ruskin may well
describe it as "a momentous and absolutely
foundational step."

CHAPTER VII.

IT is a far cry from Paternoster Row to Sunnyside, at Orpington, where Mr. Ruskin's publishing is carried on. The noise and bustle of a great
commercial establishment are exchanged for a
quiet little family circle; and instead of the
"city's central roar," you are surrounded by the
hills of Kent. The system of business presents
an even greater contrast. Other authors are
content to grumble—individually or in incorporated societies—against the wiles of publishers and the tricks of trade. Mr. Ruskin
alone has shaken himself free from the trammels,
and established a publisher and bookseller of his
own and on his own terms. This new method
was described as follows in "Fors Clavigera,"
the first of his books which bore the imprint
of "George Allen" instead of "Smith and
Elder:"—

"It costs me £10 to print 1,000 copies, and £5 more to give you a picture, and a penny off my 7*d.* to send you the book; a thousand sixpences are £25; when you have bought a thousand 'Fors' of me I shall therefore have £5 for my trouble, and my single shopman, Mr. Allen, £5 for his; we won't work for less, either of us. And I mean to sell all my large books, henceforward, in the same way; well printed, well bound, and at a fixed price; and the trade may charge a proper and acknowledged profit for their trouble in retailing the book. Then the public will know what they are about, and so will tradesmen. I, the first producer, answer, to the best of my power, for the quality of the book—paper, binding, eloquence, and all: the retail dealer charges what he ought to charge, openly; and if the public do not choose to give it, they can't get the book. That is what I call legitimate business."

It is now sixteen years since Mr. Ruskin started this plan of campaign, and in view of the ever-recurring controversy between authors and publishers, I sought an opportunity a year or two ago of learning how the plan is found to work. Mr. George Allen inquired for Mr. Ruskin's wishes in the matter, and Mr. Ruskin kindly authorized him to tell me "everything I cared to ask, and show me everything I cared to see." The following, with such alterations only as have been necessary to bring the particulars up to date, was the description, written at the time, of what is probably one of the most successful publishing businesses of the day :— ·

"Mr. Ruskin has transferred his publishing," said the trade circular contemptuously, some years ago, "to the middle of a country field." The remark was quite true. Sunnyside is a pleasant private house, standing in its own grounds, which slope down into one of the prettiest vales of Kent. Mr. Allen tells me that he is fond of roses, and the fame of his cabbages is known to readers of "Fors Clavigera." The place is only some twelve miles from London, but the scene is one of complete rural seclusion. Like his principal, Mr. Allen has his thorn in the flesh, for one uncompromisingly ugly cottage is visible to the right ; but with this exception the view from the drawing-room windows stretches uninterruptedly over the vale to the Knockholt Beeches. On one of the walls there hangs, between some pencil drawings by Mr. Ruskin of his favourite Abbeville, a water-colour drawing of the view which Mr. Ruskin sees from his study window. It is drawn by Mr. Ruskin, and shows "morning breaking along the Coniston Fells, and the mists, motionless and grey beneath the rose of the moorlands, veiling the lower woods, and the sleeping village, and the long lawns by the lake-shore."

Behind Mr. Allen's house, at one side of his back garden, stands a substantial building which serves for warehouse. It is a valuable one. "I have taken stock only recently, and I find we have £28,000 worth of goods stowed away. You see our business was not made ; it grew. If I had foreseen its growth I should have built a more commodious warehouse, but we began in a humble way without one at all, and I cannot go on adding to it, or I should cover my garden in no time ; so we have to utilize every inch of space, as you see ; up there is 'The Stones of Venice ;' down there in the corner is 'The Seven Lamps of Architecture.'" If the science of architecture consists in the adjustment of means to end, Mr. Ruskin's publisher has lit his author's lamps to some purpose, for a neater and better-kept warehouse you will not easily find. There are sixty-three different works (or editions) of Mr. Ruskin's in stock, most of them in various styles of binding. To keep all these in due place, so as to execute orders for one here and there every day, in what is hardly more than a garden outhouse, requires considerable skill. And then Mr. Ruskin's books are not like other people's, which are complete in one volume, or two volumes, or three. He has at least a dozen of them on hand, appearing in parts, at irregular intervals—a method which calls for quite as much method on the publisher's part as versatility on the author's.

The issuing department is as heavily taxed as the stockkeeping. Ordinary publishers deal, of course, almost entirely wholesale. Most of their books are sub-scribed for by the trade, and subsequent country orders are concentrated by London middlemen. But Mr. Ruskin's leading idea was to eliminate the middleman. His agent is bookseller and publisher in one. The books are "published by," and for a long time were only "to be had of, Mr. George Allen, Sunnyside, Orpington." This, of course, entails a great deal of labour upon the central establishment, which in the ordinary course of the trade is divided among many hands. As Mr. Ruskin's books are all sumptuously got up, so they have to be all carefully packed. Every parcel is protected by straw or deal boards, and the sorting, packing, tying, weighing, and stamping make up a good day's work for all concerned. Her Majesty's Post-master-General sucks no small advantage therefrom, but he affords no special facilities, and every afternoon Mr. Allen's man may be seen trudging off with his bundles on his back to the village post-office, a mile and more distant from Sunnyside. The bundles are heavy, but the result is not cumbrous. There was a great run on the new edition of "The Stones of Venice," but every subscriber had his copy or copies despatched within four days of publication. "Præterita," too, is very popular, but each part is punctually delivered within three days. In one respect, however, Mr. Ruskin's method greatly eases his publisher's labour. "Mr. Allen has positive orders to attend to no letter asking credit." This rule is not quite strictly enforced as against the trade. Obviously a bookseller could not be expected to pay for twenty copies, say, of "The Stones of Venice," at four guineas each, before delivery, but prompt payment is expected and is made, and in the case of private customers credit is very seldom allowed. The accounts at the Orpington establishment—which Mr. Allen was good enough to place unreservedly in my hands—are comparatively simple, and what is more, are capable, of course, of being always kept close up to date. The value of every book disposed of is also immediately credited, and Mr. Ruskin's balance-sheet can therefore at any moment be precisely made up to the exact date. How many authors, I wonder, are in an equally fortunate condition !

The readers will probably be surprised, I think, to hear what the staff is which discharges the various duties I have described. It consists of eight persons only, two of whom, it should be stated, are largely occupied not so much in the publishing as in the producing department. Mr. Allen himself is an engraver by profession. For thirty years he has been engaged as Mr. Ruskin's assistant in this matter. Readers of "Modern Painters" will remember Mr. Ruskin's compliment to "Mr. G. Allen's accurate line studies from nature," and nearly all his later works— from the Oxford lectures to "Præterita"—have been engraved by the same careful and skilful hands. Mr. Allen, in his turn, is assisted in the engraving work by his second son. The eldest son and daughter are chiefly responsible for directing the details of the publishing work, while the remaining members of the family are the other "hands." Even so, I have not enumerated all the family tasks. More and more Mr. Ruskin has come, as he has said, to trust to his good friends at Orpington. At first he took an active part in superintending the issue of his books ; but latterly he has merely said, " Bring out such and such a book," and they bring it out ; " Do this," and they do it. Miss Allen, in addition to her duties as proof-reader, was mainly responsible, too, for the compilation of the " Ruskin Birthday Book." " Is not the establishment rather heavily taxed," I asked, " at times, when a new book, like ' The Stones of Venice,' for instance, is issued?" " Well, yes, it is," was the answer ; " but what we have to do, we do. For one thing, there is no alternative. You see there is nobody in this village whom we could take on for emergencies ; but besides that, we all have our hearts in the work, and have been determined from the first to make Mr. Ruskin's experiment a success." Publishing at Orpington is, it will be seen,

distinctly a home industry, and the Allens, as Mr.
Ruskin says, in the Preface to the 1880 edition of " The
Seven Lamps of Architecture," are distinctly "a help-
ful family."

Visitors to Sunnyside are not unnaturally a good
deal surprised. "Generally," I was told, "they will not
believe it is the right house. They apologise for their
mistake; they wanted 'the shop;' will we kindly
direct them to 'Allen's'?" "And have you had distinguished strangers among your customers, who have
come in person?" "Not very many. Mr. Darwin used
to live a mile or two off, and members of his family
came sometimes. Carlyle, too, came over once, when
he was staying at Lord Derby's place at Keston. He
was very interesting, and wanted particularly to know
whether we didn't keep 'a coo.'" (It was after this
visit, no doubt, that Carlyle wrote to Emerson of
"the way Ruskin has towards the bibliopolic world.")
"Visitors seldom understand that we can have any
work to do. The greatest sceptic of all is Mr. Ruskin
himself. When he was staying with us last year we
tried to get him to come and help; but he was quite
frightened at the parcels, and refused to believe that
anybody really wanted to buy his books. We must
take him for walks, he said, and so off we girls went
with him to the flowers and the woods."

The foregoing report will show that Mr.
Ruskin's new departure in publishing has, at
any rate, carried out in practice two favourite
ideals of the "New Political Economy:" it has
established a happy village industry, and it has

partially eliminated the middleman. How far
it has succeeded in securing authors' profits and
preventing "underselling" by the trade (for
all Mr. Ruskin's books are retailed at their
published prices, a fixed discount being allowed
to the trade) will be seen from the following
details, which Mr. Allen gave me respecting his
sales and dealings, both with Mr. Ruskin and
with the trade :—

"I could even sell my books," said Mr. Ruskin ten
years ago in "Fors," "for not inconsiderable sums of
money if I chose to bribe the reviewers, pay half of all
I get to the booksellers, stick bills on the lamp-posts,
and say nothing but what would please the Bishop of
Peterborough. I could say a great deal that would
please him, and yet be very good and useful ; I should
like much again to be on terms with my old publisher,
and hear him telling me nice stories over our walnuts,
this Christmas, after dividing his year's spoil with me
in Christmas charity." Remembering this passage, and
others of about the same date, in which Mr. Ruskin
spoke, at the outset of his campaign against the
publishing and bookselling trades, of the sacrifices it
entailed on him, I asked Mr. Allen how the fortune
of war had gone since then. "It has been a winning
game," said Mr. Allen, "and a gradually expanding
business. It began sixteen years ago with Mr. Ruskin
employing me to sell 'Fors Clavigera.' His original
battle was against the bookselling trade only. Messrs.
Smith and Elder printed 'Fors' at first, and I sold

them. Mr. Ruskin objected to the principle of discounts and abatements adopted by the booksellers, and I was to sell 'Fors' at a fixed price to all comers. Then came the 'Revised Series' of his already completed works ('Sesame and Lilies,' etc.); these originally bore the double imprint of Messrs. Smith, Elder, and Co. and myself. They were sold—in purple calf bindings only—in both cases, on the same terms as 'Fors.' After 1873 Mr. Ruskin's connection with his old publishers ceased, and he gradually threw all his publishing on me. Since then I have undertaken publishing for other authors besides Mr. Ruskin. I am an engraver, and had no special knowledge of the publishing trade whatever. But the business has grown and grown ever since."

"Till it has reached—what?" "Well, Mr. Ruskin has instructed me to tell you everything you care to ask, so I shall break no confidence if I show you these accounts. For instance, from the new edition of 'The Stones of Venice' Mr. Ruskin has received already £1,583 clear profits, besides leaving 1,272 copies unpaid for."* "Is that his greatest success?" "I cannot say yet, for the edition was only published last year. So far, I think, 'The Seven Lamps of Architecture' has done best. The author's clear profits from the editions I have published of that book have amounted to close upon £2,500.† But without going into further details, I may tell you that last year (1886) I was able to pay over to Mr. Ruskin, as his profit,

* Mr. Ruskin's profit on the new edition of "Stones of Venice" up to the end of 1889 was altogether £3,069, i.e., since the book was published, in 1886.

† £3,200 between 1880 and 1889.

N

£4,000. And to that you should add the fact that during the year we greatly increased the value of his stock—as, for instance, by the new edition of 'The Stones of Venice.' We have paid all the cost of production, and the profits on it will come steadily in." It will be seen that Mr. Ruskin's royalties, if one puts his profits that way, are extraordinarily large. Thus, 2000 copies of the "Seven Lamps," at £1, 1s., brought him a clear profit of £991, equivalent to a royalty of 10s. a copy. And this, so far as I examined, was about the average rate. Thus, to take a cheaper book, I noticed that 3000 copies of "Sesame and Lilies," at 5s., brought him in £345.

"And what, if I may ask, is your own arrangement as publisher with Mr. Ruskin?" "I first published for him simply on commission. This arrangement lasted till the end of 1886. Since then I have worked under an agreement for proportionate profits."

"You have given me some figures of the profits on various books; can you give me any of the sales, to show their comparative popularity?" Mr. Allen readily complied with my request, and drew up the following table showing the sales during 1886 of some of the more popular of Mr. Ruskin's books :—

	Volumes.[*]
"Sesame and Lilies" (small edition).	2,122
"Frondes Agrestes".	1,273
"The Stones of Venice" (large edition) first half-year of issue	939
"Unto This Last"	874

[*] For 1889 the figures are 2,902, 1,038, 218, 775, 703, 503, 514, 334, 613, 105, 298.

	Volumes.
" Ethics of the Dust " .	808
" Fors Clavigera " (volumes of) .	730
" The Seven Lamps of Architecture ".	668
" Modern Painters," Vol. II. (small edition)	652
" The Stones of Venice " (small travellers' edition, in two vols.), each	675
" On the Old Road," first year .	597
" King of the Golden River "	388

The " King of the Golden River," it may be interesting to add, is largely bought by the London and Sheffield School Boards for Prizes. Mr. Ruskin's " Letter to Young Girls " has also a large sale, 264 packets (containing 3,168 copies in all) having been sold during last year (1886).

With regard to the " Revised Series " of Mr. Ruskin's works, the following were the sales during 1886 :—

" Sesame and Lilies " .	272
" The Crown of Wild Olive "	188
" The Queen of the Air"	108
" The Eagle's Nest " .	104
" The Two Paths "	96
" Time and Tide "	89
" Munera Pulveris "	73
* " Val d'Arno "	54
* " Aratra Pentelici "	53
" 'A Joy for Ever'"	51
* " Ariadne Florentina "	40

This series, it should be stated, is a very expensive one, the ordinary volumes costing 13s. each (unbound), the illustrated (marked above with an asterisk) 22s. 6d. These volumes are, however, all in course of being issued in cheap form, similar to the small "Sesame and Lilies."

From the sales the conversation turned to the buyers. "Where," I asked, "do your customers come from?" "From all parts of the kingdom, but more from Scotland and the north than from the south, excepting London. It is a curious fact, too, that I send very much fewer books to Oxford than to Cambridge; a prophet is of no honour, I suppose, in his own university. The circulating libraries do not patronize us at all, with the exception of Mudie's, which takes perhaps fifty of each of the smaller works in the course of the year. Lately the orders from the Continent and the colonies (especially Australia) have very much increased." "America, I suppose, lives on its pirated editions." "Yes, and tries to export them sometimes. I remember we were lately asked, as a special favour, to pass through a set of American editions for a celebrated traveller. The matter was referred to Mr. Ruskin, who replied that 'Mr. —— had much better not burden himself with stolen property on his missionary expedition. He shall certainly not do so with permission of mine.'"

Since the foregoing pages were first written, the new edition of "Modern Painters" has been published. This was the biggest job by far that his present publisher has undertaken. The money value of the edition, at its retail price, was not far short of £20,000. The weight of

the special hand-made copies was over six tons.
The publication of any book of these dimensions
would be a heavy undertaking; but "Modern
Painters" is a portfolio of engravings, as well
as a library of literature.   It is the most important of all Mr. Ruskin's literary works, but
it was also, in its original form, one of the most
elaborate and beautiful collections of illustrations ever issued.   Mr. Allen was responsible,
not only for the republication of the book, but
for the reissue of these illustrations, compris-
ing eighty-seven full-page engravings and over
200 woodcuts.   Such an undertaking would
obviously put to a crucial test the interesting
experiment in publishing which Mr. Ruskin
initiated now nearly twenty years ago.   I ap-
pend, therefore, to what has already been said
this further description of a second visit paid
to Orpington, in January, 1889 :—

I found the house and household taxed to its utter-
most by the new enterprise.   Indeed, a new room had
been specially added to the premises to stock the copies
of this bulky book.   Nothing in any of the largest publishing houses could excel the neatness and precision
of the arrangements.   Indeed, the new warehouse in
this country villa on the Kentish hills reminded me of
nothing so much as some careful housewife's linen·

closet—only that the sheets were the sheets of a book. And just as in a well-ordered household each member has a daily task marked out, so here each member of Mr. Allen's helpful family has his share, or hers, in the work of publishing. As I glanced round at the piles of "Modern Painters" (each set of six volumes weighing 29 lbs.) I thought it would be hard on the packer. Every one was going to lend him a hand, but even so it had been found necessary for once to bring in outside help, and two men from London were employed in doing up the parcels for distribution, which left in special vans, direct by road, to the principal booksellers. "Modern Painters" will thus be Ruskinian to the end, and every devout purchaser in London will have the satisfaction of knowing that his copy came by road, and not by rail.

But indeed "the Master's" ideals have been adhered to throughout in the production of this final edition of his chief work. "About the plates I shall have plenty to tell you presently," said Mr. Allen ; "but first let me say that the binding has been done by my usual binder, Mr. Mansell ; I need not add that there is no machine-stitching about it, but only honest hand-work. With regard to the printing of the letterpress, the New York *Critic* remarked the other day that ' there was something very attractive in the idea of this printing-house in the fields, far from the city's rush and roar. Instead of the compositor snatching a hasty lunch at his case, with the smell of the inky rollers in his nostrils and the noise of the stone-paved streets in his ears, he may step outside of the composing-room into a rose-perfumed garden at Orpington, and munch his meal with no noise to disturb him save that of the busy bees or the babbling brook. And how much better work he can do amid

such surroundings ! No wonder that Ruskin's books
are so beautifully printed !' As applied to us here,
this is of course incorrect, for my printing is all done
by Messrs. Hazell, Watson, and Viney, at Aylesbury ;
but in substance the New York writer was not far wrong.
Messrs. Hazell's place at Aylesbury is quite an ideal
printing-office—with light and cheerful buildings, allot-
ment gardens, recreation-ground, clubs, a magazine,
and all the other machinery for 'mutual improvement.'
You may care to know, by the way, that this edition of
' Modern Painters ' took over 600 reams of paper for the
ordinary copies ; they are printed on specially made
toned paper, of fine surface but tough texture, which
weighed in all well over fifteen tons. The hand-made
paper for the special copies was also made by Whatman
expressly for this book, and is of a size and weight
never before manufactured. The type, too, was a special
fount, cast expressly for this work, and indeed the
printing has, I may say, been done throughout quite
regardless of cost."

"This is even more the case," continued Mr. Allen,
"with regard to the printing of the plates. Mr. Robert
Smith, to whom I entrusted the work, is an out-and-out
good and honest workman. Curiously enough, he was
an apprentice to the printer who did the original edition
for Messrs. Smith and Elder, and he was as anxious as
I to get the best possible results from each plate. I do
not know where else I could have gone to get equally
good work, for Mr. Smith is a workman himself, and
gives close and continuous personal superintendence.
Even so, some of the delay in publishing the book has
been due to the difficulty of finding a sufficient number
of conscientious workmen. Such men are never over-
abundant, and a great many of them have been drawn

off by Professor Herkomer to his workshops at Bushey. However, I have not stinted Mr. Smith in the price, and that is the main essential. You have no idea of the tricks to which plate-printers often resort—and necessarily—owing to the cutting down of the price : the mixture of soft soap with the ink is one way—so a workman told me himself—in which time is saved and the work scamped."

From the printing of the plates the conversation turned to the preparation of the plates themselves, and here the curious may be glad of some detailed particulars. The plates in the new edition of " Modern Painters " may be divided under four heads—(1) new plates, not included in any previous edition ; (2) plates of which the originals have been destroyed, and which have been re-engraved for the present edition ; (3) plates in a like case which have been mechanically reproduced ; and (4) original plates retouched. The *additional plates* are three in number, and it is these which will always give an unique value among collectors to the present edition. The subjects of them are " Château de Blois," " Dawn after the Wreck," and " Lake of Zug." They were all etched by Mr. Ruskin in 1859, from Turner's drawings, and engraved by T. Lupton. Intended for the fifth volume, they were held back owing to the anxiety of Mr. Ruskin's father to see the work fairly off his son's hands. The *re-engraved plates* are nine in number, and include some of the best-known illustrations in the book, such as " The Lombard Apennine " and " Monte Rosa." Three other plates had also been destroyed, but Mr. Allen fortunately had in his possession early proofs of the original etchings, and from these *photogravures* have been executed for the present edition by the Goupil process (Messrs.

Boussod, Valadon, and Co.). "Finally, the remaining plates have all been looked to," said Mr. Allen, "with loving care by myself and my son (Mr. Hugh Allen) both in retouching where necessary, and also in superintendence of printing."

Into the merits of the new edition of " Modern Painters " I need not enter, for most of my readers have no doubt formed an opinion of their own by personal inspection. But in concluding this description of Mr. Ruskin's system of publication, and with it—for the present at least—my survey of his work in some of its aspects, it will not be out of place to record that the edition has been a great commercial success. Mr. Ruskin's profits from this one issue of a single book will not in the end be less than £6,000. Hitherto he has suffered badly from the American pirates. Though his American readers are numbered by tens of thousands, he has never received a penny from them ; but the cheaper editions of many of his books which Mr. Allen is now bringing out will doubtless do something to undermine the pirates' trade. But even now Mr. Ruskin's profits are steadily growing every year, and exceed, I imagine, those made by any other serious author of the time.

His system of publishing " in the wilds of Kent "
has—like most other schemes of his devising—
been derided as unpractical, visionary, and mad.
On closer inspection does there not seem to be
some method in Mr. Ruskin's mad work ?

APPENDICES

CONTAINING NOTES ON MR. RUSKIN'S
OXFORD LECTURES.

APPENDIX I.

THE first course of Lectures which I heard Mr. Ruskin deliver at Oxford was one given in Michaelmas term, 1877. The lectures, which he called "Readings in 'Modern Painters,'" were conversational and informal; and the following notes embody only some casual reminiscences. As, however, the lectures were thoroughly characteristic of their author, even my imperfect notes may be of interest to some readers.*

The three great principles of Art are, Mr.

* Writing at the end of this course to Miss Beever, Mr. Ruskin said, "I write first to you this morning to tell you that I gave yesterday the twelfth and last of my course of lectures, this term, to a room crowded by six hundred people, two-thirds members of the University, and with its door wedged open by those who could not get in; this interest of theirs being granted to me, I doubt not, because for the first time in Oxford I have been able to speak to them boldly of immortal life. I intended when I began the course only to have read 'Modern Painters' to them; but when I began, some of your favourite bits interested the men so much, and brought so much larger a proportion of undergraduates than usual, that I took pains to re-inforce and press them home; and people say I have never given so useful a course yet" ("Hortus Inclusus," p. 47).

Ruskin said, these: *First*, that the life of Art is in Religion; *secondly*, its food, in the ocular and passionate love of nature; *thirdly*, its health, in the humility of the artists. To these three essential Truths he went on to oppose three popular Fallacies, corresponding to them; namely, *first*, that the life of Art is in Sensuality; *secondly*, its food, in the telescopic and dispassionate examination of nature; and *thirdly*, its health, in the pride and riches of the artist. In architecture, too, the lecturer laid down three canons; namely, *first*, that the material should be good and true; *secondly*, the ornament, natural; and *thirdly*, the designer left free to work from his heart.

"Readings from 'Modern Painters'" led to few opportunities for enlarging on these architectural canons, and the major part of the lecturer's running commentary was devoted to illustrating one or other of the three Principles of Art. More especially did the lecturer's mind appear to be running on the artistic, as opposed to the scientific way of viewing nature. The true artist, he said, if he wishes to paint a dog, looks at him and loves him; now we vivisect him. Yet true science—true knowledge of any living creature—begins in the love of it, not in dissection. The mere sight of this museum (see p. 49), he said, with its specimens of death and disease, instead of life and health, paralyzes me in all artistic work. The fact is, though modern science forgets it, that sight is spiritual as well as physical. The pleasure of modern science

is the pride of seeing more by instruments than
common people can with the naked eye. Of
the two dominant schools in the University, one
despises Nature, the other despises God. Man's
eye sees through his soul. But nowadays sight
has become mechanical. Instead of learning to
sketch, we buy photographs; instead of loving
the poets, we try to imitate them. Natural
Philosophy exultingly hopes to be able to turn
on God; and already we read of a tolling
machine erected in Ealing Cemetery, at a cost
of £80, the sexton, like a miller at his dam,
turning on lamentation.

Students of Mr. Ruskin's works will remember many passages in which several of the
aphorisms thrown out in these Oxford Lectures
have been expanded or illustrated; and I pass
now to one or two notes on the third Principle
of Art laid down above. The health of Art
consists in the humility of the artist. I have
in my possession, said Mr. Ruskin, Turner's
receipt for £28, 7s., paid for three drawings of
Florence. One of these would now fetch from
£500 to £800. The high prices now paid for
pictures are the cause of the hurry in modern
work. A man can resist a bribe of nine guineas,
but not so easily one of £2,000. Even here in
Oxford the leaven of pride and riches is at work.
The peace of Isis is disturbed by shouts of
ambition, and all ambition is shameful. No
natural beauty can be seen through a shameful
passion. It was want of compassion, said Mr.
Ruskin, which often made me fail to appreciate

Turner's work, for he painted always in pity
or joy.

The illustration from his earlier writings of
the Principles of Art above described was one
of the threads which kept together this discursive course of " Readings in ' Modern Painters.'"
Another was the explanation of the origin and
object of that great book.   The first volume of
it was, he said, an expansion of a long letter in
defence of Turner. About 1840 a marked change
took place in Turner's style.   The change is to
be seen in the " Rivers of France," and was from
yellow and grey to truth in colour.   The central
idea of the defence of Turner, as contained in
" Modern Painters," was that sight depends on
the soul, and that, said Mr. Ruskin, I have shown
you to be entirely true.   But I wanted more
knowledge to make the essay really effective,
and by the time I had got the knowledge the
period of public reprobation had begun.   I am
ashamed now of the affected style of the volume.
Subsequently I read Carlyle, and succeeded in
catching something of his rhythm. I am ashamed
too of my pretended systems.   Plato, added Mr.
Ruskin, in an excursus at this point, threw out
systems like the gleam on foam; Herbert Spencer
throws them out like boys blowing bubbles full
of dirty air.   After all, my system only amounted
to this : " The picture must be done well, the
thing must be pretty, and the motive good."
My denial, in the first volume, of the delight
in " ideas of power" was wrong too.   Venera-
tion, desire for exertion, and sympathy are all

involved in "ideas of power," and are all legitimate elements of delight.

This self-criticism of "Modern Painters" was afterwards written down by Mr. Ruskin in the new edition of the second volume. But in these Oxford Lectures it was carried out with a bantering humour of which no notes can convey much impression. I remember in particular one lecture which, setting out from a criticism of passages in some of his earlier books, resolved itself into a discourse upon style. He read to us first the passage from the "Seven Lamps"—one of the best known of his "purple patches"—which I have already quoted (see p. 17). With this passage he bade us compare the following from "Unto This Last," which he read with fervid emphasis :—

"And if, on due and honest thought over these things, it seems that the kind of existence to which men are now summoned, by every plea of pity and claim of right, may, for some time at least, not be a luxurious one ; consider whether, even supposing it guiltless, luxury would be desired by any of us, if we saw clearly at our sides the suffering which accompanies it in the world. Luxury is indeed possible in the future—innocent and exquisite ; luxury for all, and by the help of all ; but luxury at present can only be enjoyed by the ignorant ; the cruellest man living could not sit at his feast, unless he sat blindfold. Raise the veil boldly ; face the light ; and if, as yet, the light of the eye can only be through tears, and the light of the body through sackcloth, go thou forth weeping, bearing precious seed, until the time come, and the kingdom, when Christ's gift of bread and bequest of peace shall be *unto this last* as unto thee ; and when, for earth's severed multitudes of the wicked and the weary, there shall be holier reconciliation than that of the narrow home, and calm economy, where the Wicked cease—not from trouble, but from troubling—and the Weary are at rest."

Compare those two passages carefully, he said, and you will know for ever afterwards the difference between bad and good style. Note in particular, he added, first, that the art which in the earlier passage is obvious at every point is in the later one hardly visible at all : *ars est cclare artem ;* and secondly, that no word in the later passage could be changed without loss of meaning. There is, indeed, one alliteration ("*p*lea of *p*ity"), but the word plea was the inevitably right word in its place. In my early works I used to hunt about for alliterations for their own sake. What makes Carpaccio's art so great—Carpaccio had recently been discovered by Mr. Ruskin as the greatest of painters, and there were several passing allusions to him in these lectures—is that it is hidden.

I find among my notes—scattered and discursive, even as were the lectures—the following few disjointed aphorisms and sentences which may be set down as they come :—

Science is bad English which vanishes when it is translated.

The modern stage is ruined by its realization of scenery, which is contrary to all noble art. A picture, whether on canvas or on the stage, should give an idea, not its realization.

Stacy Marks has produced the first perfect pictures of birds ; Copley Fielding produced the best picture of a moor ; Burne-Jones is our only living real artist.

We can only discern spiritual nature so far as we are like it.

To speak of "natural" and "supernatural" is like calling the organic "super-mineral."

APPENDIX II. -

THE second complete course of Mr. Ruskin's
Oxford Lectures which I had the privilege of
attending was the one on " The Art of England."
Of these I took full notes at the time, for publication in the *Pall Mall Gazette*; but the lectures
had been carefully prepared, and the printed
volume differs very little from the spoken
lectures. There would, therefore, be no point
in republishing my notes. With the lectures
entitled "The Pleasures of England," which I
similarly reported, the case is different. The
course had clearly not been so carefully prepared, nor was the lecturer's line of thought so
closely reasoned, as in "The Art of England."
My reports took the form, therefore, of "digested
plans" (so Mr. Ruskin was kind enough to call
them), "summarizing a line of thought not always by me enough expressed, and completing
and illustrating it from other parts of my books,
often more fully than, against time, I could do
myself." Accordingly I reprint these reports
here in their original form, in the hope that

they may be found by a reader here and there
to serve as useful companions to the printed
lectures.

LECTURE I.

"BERTHA TO OSBURGA: THE PLEASURES
OF LEARNING."

(*Pall Mall Gazette*, October 20th, 1884.)

THE course of lectures which Mr. Ruskin proposes to give in Oxford this term, and the first
of which was delivered on Saturday, is intended
to trace in rough outline the whole history of
England as written in her art.

The Future of England.

Mr. Ruskin's history, it need hardly be said,
has a purpose and a moral; and the object of
his survey of English art is, he stated at the outset on Saturday, to show what those of us who
have faculty should do, and those of us who have
sensibility should admire. "Such action and
such feeling may even yet create a future for
England which all of you may hopefully and
proudly labour for, and some of you even see,
when all the tumult of vain avarice and idle
pleasure has gone to its appointed perdition."
Wherein his hope for the future of England
lies Mr. Ruskin expounded in eloquent words,
written several years ago, which, as being "the

most pregnant and essential" of all his professorial teachings, he repeated on Saturday :—

"There is a destiny now possible to us—the highest
ever set before a nation to be accepted or refused. We
are still undegenerate in race : a race mingled of the
best northern blood. We are not yet dissolute in temper, but still have the firmness to govern and the grace
to obey. We have been taught a religion of pure mercy,
which we must either now finally betray, or learn to defend by fulfilling. And we are rich in an inheritance of
honour, bequeathed to us through a thousand years of
noble history, which it should be our daily thirst to increase with splendid avarice, so that Englishmen, if it
be a sin to covet honour, should be the most offending
souls alive. Within the last few years we have had the
laws of natural science opened to us with a rapidity
which has been blinding by its brightness ; and means
of transit and communication given to us, which have
made but one kingdom of the habitable globe. One
kingdom ;—but who is to be its king ? Is there to be no
king in it, think you, and every man to do that which is
right in his own eyes ? or only kings of terror, and the
obscene empires of Mammon and Belial ? Or will you,
youths of England, make your country again a royal
throne of kings ; a sceptred isle ; for all the world a
source of light, a centre of peace : mistress of Learning
and of the Arts ; faithful guardian of great memories, in
the midst of irreverent and ephemeral visions ; faithful
servant of time-tried principles, under temptation from
fond experiments and licentious desires ; and amidst
the cruel and clamorous jealousies of the nations, worshipped in her strange valour, of goodwill towards
men ?"

History Written in Art.

Fifteen years have passed since Mr. Ruskin
wrote those words, and he has not lost hope in

the interval; on the contrary, he is more than
ever convinced that there has been "no time,
in all the pride of the past, when their country
might more serenely trust in the glory of her
youth, when her prosperity was more secure in
their genius, or her honour in their hearts."
What, then, are the young men and maidens of
England to do to carry out these hopes ? That
may best be learned, said Mr. Ruskin, by considering whether London be indeed "the natural
and Divinely appointed produce of the valley of
the Thames;" and if not, how far it may be
altered by our acts and our thoughts. Mr.
Ruskin has said before (in his preface to the
translation of Xenophon's "Economics" in
"Bibliotheca Pastorum") that all right education should include the history of five cities—
Athens, Rome, Venice, Florence, and London.
The history of Athens, rightly understood,
teaches all that we need to know of the religion
and art of Greece; that of Rome, the victory of
Christianity over barbarism; that of Venice and
Florence, all that is essential in Christianity, as
illustrated by Christian painting, sculpture, and
architecture; that of London, with its sister
Paris, Christian chivalry expressed in Gothic
architecture. Mr. Ruskin had once hoped to
write the history of these five cities, and it is
the history of London, understood in this manner, that he proposes to tell in the present
course of lectures—the history, that is to say,
of the English and French nations, as expounded
in their architecture, their illuminated manu-

scripts, and, in a minor degree, their jewellery
and other lesser arts. The change in the title
of his lectures is significant of this historical
purpose. "Hitherto in all my writings I have
considered art solely in relation to the personal
temper of the artist, and so I have simply told
you that you ought to like Turner and dislike
Salvator Rosa, without ever considering what
your own instinct or genius would prompt you
to like or dislike. In this course Art is to be
looked at throughout from the people's side; it
is to be asked what, as a matter of fact, they
did like; and hence I have called my lectures
'The Pleasures of England,' instead of, as before, 'The Art of England.'"

"*Learning*" and "*Teaching*" Nations.

First in historical order among these pleasures
comes the pleasure of learning—the pleasure,
that is, not of seeking truth for oneself, which
is a completely different thing, but of receiving
instruction—a pleasure which to all who have
the grace to receive is extremely sweet and
sacred. It is a pleasure, though, Mr. Ruskin
here interposed, which can hardly find a place
in your modern theories, "according to which
you turn out what you are to be by the inevitable operation of what is within you; whereas
the old theory of education was that the baby
material was by external force and wisdom bred
—that it was a plastic vase, to be shaped and
mannered as the potter chose, not as it chose,

until it was filled with sweetness of sound doc-
trine, like Hybla honey or Arabian spikenard."
Now, Athens and Rome were essentially self-
taught cities, but London and Paris are essentially taught by others : —

"You find, from the earliest times, in Greece and Italy
a multitude of artists gradually perfecting the knowledge and representation of the human body, glorified
by the exercises of war.   You have, north of Greece and
Italy, innumerable and incorrigibly savage nations,
representing, with rude and irregular efforts, on huge
stones and ice-borne boulders, on cave bones and forest
stocks and logs, with any manner of innocent tinting
or scratching possible to them, sometimes beasts, sometimes hobgoblins, sometimes Heaven only knows
what, but never attaining any skill in figure-drawing
until, whether invading or invaded, Greece and Italy
teach them what a human being is like; and with that
help they dream and blunder on through the centuries,
achieving many fantastic and amusing things, more
especially the art of rhyming, whereby they usually
express their notions of things far better than by painting.   Nevertheless, in due course we get a Holbein
out of them ; and in the end, far best product hitherto,
Sir Joshua, and the supremely Gothic Gainsborough.

By "supremely Gothic Gainsborough" Mr. Ruskin explained that he meant, not that Gainsborough painted " kings and saints turning up
their eyes, such as you buy at so much a hundred, wherewith to ornament your pseudo-Gothic
temples," but that in his portraits the face was
everything, the body nothing, whereas the glory
of classic art is always in the body, and never
in the face.   The foregoing summary of English
art may, Mr. Ruskin added, be still further

condensed in Carlylean phrase; and the art of
England may be said to consist of three whales'
cubs combined by boiling under the orders of
the Athena of Homer and Phidias.*

Untaught British Art.

Mr. Ruskin then proceeded to summarize
shortly the characteristics of the learning and
teaching nations respectively.   The Huns and
Vandals he passed over, as being merely "forms
of punishment and destruction," and came to
immortal nations living on their native rocks
and unchanging plains.   Of the learning nations,
the British have the deepest love of external
nature, of pure music and song; they were
deeply religious, but neither apprehensive nor
receptive.   "I do not speak of the Celtic race,"

---

* "Mr. Ruskin incidentally referred again on Saturday
(wrote the *Pall Mall Gazette* a fortnight later) to those
'three whales' cubs combined by boiling' which the *Saturday Review* found so hard a saying as only to be accepted
on our authority.   It is a pretty compliment, but one which
we cannot accept, that our imprimatur is necessary to give
currency to a phrase of Carlyle's.   Mr. Ruskin was quoting,
of course, from *Friedrich*, where Carlyle describes how the
Wends 'set up their god Triglaph—a three-headed mon-
ster of which I have seen prints, beyond measure ugly—
something like *three whales' cubs combined by boiling* or a
triple porpoise dead drunk.'   The Wends were at this time
(A.D. 1023) 'sturdy heathens,' and their representation of
Triglaph was very appropriately, therefore, taken by Mr.
Ruskin as typical of the Northern art, which was subsequently to be touched through Christianity by 'the spear
of Pallas.'"

Mr. Ruskin said, "because I should now be expected to say Keltic, and I don't mean to, if only for fear that I should next be required to say St. Kckilia." The Normans were scarcely more apprehensive, but had more constructive energy, their chief characteristic being that they never spend themselves in vain anger, or passion, or sorrow; they are like the living rock, they flow like lava, and congeal like granite. The Saxons and Franks are docile, imaginative, and active, but with difficulty rational, and rarely wise. For the type of the Ostrogoths "you may take the German Cæsars, still standing as a barrier against the license and insolence of modern Republican Governments." And lastly, there are the Lombards, sternly indocile, gloomily imaginative; for the Lombard, like the Arabian, never jests. Of British art before the people were touched by the influence of the tutor nations there is no well-sifted account; but they must have been practical builders in wood, good boat-builders, skilful in sail-weaving, with knowledge of stout ironwork and copper for ornamentation. You have here and there the stones of their temples standing one on another in the midst of deserted plains, and it is an ever-increasing matter of wonder to me that your historians never ask you to consider what you might have been if no Roman missionary had ever passed the Alps in charity, and no English king in pilgrimage; what the clay of Isis might have yielded if it had never been touched by the spear of Pallas and the rod of Agricola.

History Made Easy.

Mr. Ruskin then passed in review the chief tutor nations—"nations of which you generally learn only the corruptions, though it were better, surely, if you must choose, to learn only their virtues. For true knowledge is only of good, in which alone are nature and life ; what is diseased, and therefore unnatural, should be cut away in contemplation, as in surgery." Of these tutor nations, the Tuscan and the Arab alone had no influence on us. For the influences of the others you must look at the work of Agricola and Constantius, of Benedict and Gregory ; of the artists of Ravenna and Byzantium ; of the teaching of St. Jerome and St. Chrysostom. Of the period of history when the nations were thus learning from the Syrians, and the Greeks, and the Romans, I can give you (said Mr. Ruskin) "a few binding dates, which you will find more practically useful than the inconsequential sequences which form the index of common histories." Another department of historical study, by the way, was considerably simplified by Mr. Ruskin, in some informal remarks, after the conclusion of his written lecture. Map-making is only tiresome when you trouble yourself about railways leading from one unimportant place to another ; but in drawing the map of England, for instance, you should put in London, and Edinburgh, and Oxford, and Lancaster, and York, and Winchester—and nothing else. With regard to the dates, from the Saxon

invasion (A.D. 449) to Alfred (A.D. 849) is a
period of exactly four hundred years. In 481
Clovis came to the throne ; and he marries Clotilde, his saint-queen, in the year (A.D. 493) in
which Theodoric wins the battle of Verona. This
is the historical conjunction which Mr. Ruskin
has described in the "Bible of Amiens:"—

"At the close of the fifth century you have Europe
divided simply by her watershed, and two Christian
kings reigning, with entirely beneficent and healthy
power—one in the north, one in the south, the mightiest
and worthiest of them married to the other's youngest
sister, a saint-queen in the north—and a devoted and
earnest woman, queen-mother, in the south. It is a conjunction of things memorable enough in the earth's history, much to be thought of, O fast-whirling reader, if
ever out of the crowd of pent-up cattle driven across
Rhine or Adige you can extricate yourself for an hour,
to walk peacefully out of the south gate of Cologne, or
across Fra Giocondo's bridge at Verona—and so, pausing, look through the clear air across the battle-field of
Tolbiac to the blue Drachenfels, or across the plain of
St. Ambrogio to the mountains of Garda. For there
were fought—if you will think closely—the two victor-
battles of the Christian world. Constantine's only gave
changed form and dying colour to the falling walls of
Rome ; but the Frank and Gothic races, thus conquering and thus ruled, founded the arts and established the
laws which gave to all future Europe her joy and her
virtue. And it is lovely to see how, even thus early, the
feudal chivalry depended for its life on the nobleness of
its womanhood. There was no vision seen, or alleged, at
Tolbiac. Clovis prayed simply to the God of Clotilde."

So too with Theodoric. His marriage with
the youngest sister of Clovis is generally dismissed in a casual sentence, as exhibiting "the

first instance of a definite policy of domestic alliances for public ends." It is not asked whether the King, who on the morning of the battle of Verona visited his mother and his sister, and "requested that on the most illustrious festival of his life they would adorn him with the rich garments which they had worked with their own hands," would be a man to marry without love; nor is it considered how far his calmly Christian justice may have been due to the sympathy and counsel of his Frankish Queen.

The Education of England in Old Times.

A hundred years later sees the marriage of Ethelbert and Bertha, signalizing the beginning of erudition and laying the corner-stone of the beautiful English character. Christianity has been accepted; faith from St. Augustine (not to be confused with the Bishop) works from the rule of Benedict—St. Augustine teaching all men what to think and feel, Benedict what to say, and be, and do; and henceforth, for three hundred years, "from Bertha to Osburga," the Saxon people are learning of the Christian faith the humane arts and duties invented and inculcated by it. This is the history which is to be found written in their art, and especially in their illuminated missals. No effect whatever can be traced on the Saxons from the luxury of Rome or from her art. They build no aqueducts or theatres; they envy no vile pleasures, and admire no classic art. The pages of a Saxon missal are the first example of the representation of immediately imagined scenes. The contest between Herakles and Hydra on a Greek vase is a mere memorandum; the potter is busy engraving his lines with due regard for the intervention of the handle. The Saxon monk scrawls his figures anywhere and everywhere all over the page, in explanatory scenes of inexpressible vision.

Modern English Missionary Enterprise.

The lesson of this page of history—the moral from past to present—is often strangely misread. The late Dean of Westminster, standing thirty years ago on St. Martin's Hill, at Canterbury, where Bertha prayed, and looking down on the cathedral where once stood the Roman church given by Ethelbert to Augustine, and on the missionary college built on the ruins of Augustine's abbey, found the prospect one of "the most inspiriting in the world;" and thinking of Augustine's solitary landing, and the subsequent missionary zeal of the people to whom he came, was minded to reflect on the mighty results which may follow from the smallest beginnings. "To this Gregorian chant in honour of the British Constitution, I grieve," said Mr. Ruskin, "but am compelled, to offer in conclusion one or two historical objections. 'From Bertha to Osburga' the Saxons were learning too eagerly to take to preaching, and whatever Christianity left these shores were not from

Thanet, but from Iona; and as for the new 'Christianized continents' that have arisen in these latter days, the missionary office of England in Africa and America has chiefly consisted in stealing lands and exterminating their inhabitants.   Our introduction of Christianity into India has only taught the natives to wear Paisley shawls instead of Cashmere; and in Australasia the 'Christian aid' that we have rendered has been principally to help pious farmers to convict labour.   And although I will take Dean Stanley's word for it that thirty years ago the prospect from St. Martin's Church was one of the cheerfullest and most inspiriting in the world, I have yet to say that recent progress has so accommodated the beauty of the surroundings to the use of the missionary works above described that the view of Canterbury Cathedral has been contracted into despised subservience to the colossal walls of an all-visible county gaol."

Lecture II.

"Alfred to the Confessor: the Pleasures of Faith."

(*Pall Mall Gazette*, October 27th, 1884.)

MR. RUSKIN prefaced the second chapter of his history on Saturday by noting two omissions:

he had to pass by the influence of the Scotch
missionaries and the whole of the Roman-British
period. The former omission he the less re-
gretted because the facts could all be found in
Montalembert's "Les Moines d'Occident," where
they could be seen better through a nimbus of
sympathetic enthusiasm than in any distortion
of them by the fog of contemptuous Rationalism.

The Roman-British Period.

Of the Roman-British period, Mr. Ruskin's
readers would find a carefully digested account
in the forthcoming number of "Our Fathers
have Told Us," entitled "Valle Crucis." Montalembert, it should be noticed, is entirely blind
to the conditions of Roman virtue which appeared in such of the Emperors as Pertinax,
Carus, or Constantius, and denies with abusive
violence the good effect of Roman law. To all
of which no better answer could be wanted than
that St. Benedict and St. Gregory were both
Roman patricians, and Imogen and Cordelia
Roman ladies. King Lear and Cymbeline both
belong to this period, and only once—when
Kent exclaims, in the first scene of the play,
" Now, by Apollo, King, Thou swear'st thy gods
in vain "—does Shakespeare throw contempt on
the Roman gods. Nor is it without significance
that the richest fighting element in the British
army to-day is to be found, not in the Saxons,
but amongst the Irish, the Highlanders, and the
Cornishmen.

The Evidence of Alfred's Penny.

Having thus completed his survey of the
sources of instruction open to our Saxon forefathers, Mr. Ruskin went on to answer the
question propounded in his first lecture, what
London would have been like if the nature of
the flowers, and trees, and children growing by
Thames-side had been rightly understood. "Of
what London was like in the days of faith I
can show you," said Mr. Ruskin, "one piece of
artistic evidence. It is Alfred's silver penny,
struck in London mint. The character of a
coinage is quite conclusive evidence in national
history, and there is no great empire in progress
but tells its story in beautiful coins. Here in
Alfred's penny—a round coin, with L. O. N. D.
I. N. I. A. struck on it—you have just the same
beauty of design, the same enigmatical arrangement of letters, as in the early inscription which
it is 'the pride of my life' to have discovered
at Venice. This inscription ('the first words
that Venice ever speaks aloud') is, it will be
remembered, on the church of S. Giacomo di
Rialto, and runs, being interpreted, 'Around
this temple let the merchant's law be just, his
weights true, and his covenants faithful.'"

A Picture of "Old London."

What the buildings of that old London were
like I cannot tell you, but at least we know that
its groups of ships and sails were exceedingly

P

beautiful. No doubt your ironclads at Portsmouth now are extremely beautiful too; but the Saxon war-ships lay at London's shore, and shone bright with banner, and shield, and dragon prow. You may be happier, but you are not handsomer, now, with your penny steamers crowded with shop-girls and shop-boys, than in the old days when "the coracles of the British tribes, the galleys of Roman armies, were moored in the Thames, and gave to London the most probable origin of its name—the City of Ships; when clear, swift rivulets, such as the Wall Brook and the Hole Bourne, descended from the higher hills through winding valleys; when the consecrated springs of Clerken Well, and Holy Well, and St. Clement's Well were the scene of many a sacred and festive pageant which gathered round their green margins." "I am quoting," said Mr. Ruskin, "from the first chapter of Dean Stanley's 'Memorials of Westminster'—a chapter which I always tell my friends who praise my writing that I would rather have written than any of my own books. But had I been able to paint so perfect a picture, the conclusions I should have drawn would have been widely different. The Dean describes, indeed, the 'river of wells' with all a poet's joy, but like a true modern citizen of Belgravia, he sees 'a quaint humour in the fact that the great arteries of our crowded streets, the vast sewers which cleanse our habitations, are fed by the life-blood of those old and living streams; that underneath our tread the Tyburn, and the

Holborn, and the Fleet, and the Wallbrook are
still pursuing their ceaseless course, still ministering to the good of man, though in a far different fashion than when Druids drank of their
sacred springs, and Saxons were baptized in
their rushing waters, ages ago.' Now, whatever
sympathy you may feel with the entire compla-
cency in the past, present, and future which is
characteristic of Dean Stanley, I would at least
beg you to observe that the transmutation of
holy wells into sewers has spoiled the Thames
as a salmon stream, from which once a year,
even as late as 1382, one of the London fisher-
men brought in a salmon for St. Peter, and took
his place beside the Prior."

Disbelief in Legends—" Solvitur Ambulando."

" Dean Stanley sees, again, in this legend of
the fish—containing the claim established by
the Abbots of Westminster on the tithe of the
Thames fisheries—an instance of ' the union of
innocent fiction with worldly craft which marks
so many legends both of Pagan and Christian
times.' A capital instance, truly, of the Lon-
donian thought which marks so many of the
well-meant books of your pious metropolis.
Let me say, in the first place, that the fiction of
old time would be no worse than that of to-day
for being innocent instead of guilty; and, in
the second place, that legends are not fictions
at all, but are the true record of impressions
brought into bright focus by action under the

impulse of faith." " Much more," continued Mr. Ruskin, " I could tell you of the reality of visions than you would believe ; but this at least I would say to you, that unless you try the rough life of Christian ages, you cannot judge of the visions or legends that resulted from it. Because you have feather beds instead of ferns for your backs, carpets instead of rushes for your feet, kickshaws instead of beef for your eating, and drains instead of holy wells for your drinking, therefore you think that you are positively the cream of creation. Stay in those pleasant circumstances and in that pleasant delusion if you will, but do not accuse your rough-fed and rough-bred forefathers of bringing back a false report from earth and sky until, like them, you have trodden the earth barefoot and looked on the heaven as they did, face to face. Do what king after king of them did—put rough shoes on your feet and walk to Rome, sleeping by the road-side when it is fine, and in the first outhouse you can find when it is wet, live, as you travel, on onions and water, and then see if you will be inclined to believe those who tell you that your experiences by the way are either poetry or fiction."

The "Stones of Westminster."

Mr. Ruskin then went on to read the history of London in the stones of Westminster Abbey —the monument of the personal character of its founder, and the shrine and throne of English faith and truth—quoting from Dean Stanley the account of Edward's vow to make a pilgrimage to the Apostle's grave; of the legend of the Hermit of Worcester, who charged the King, in the Apostle's name, to establish instead, "at Thorney, two leagues from the city," a Benedictine monastery; the legend of Edric the fisherman, and his wonderful encounter with St. Peter; and finally the two miracles (of the cure of the cripple, and of the child appearing in the sacramental elements to the King Leofric and Godiva), which still further endeared the little chapel of St. Peter to the Confessor. After describing the architecture and plan of Edward's Abbey, Mr. Ruskin read, for purposes of subsequent deprecation, Stanley's general reflections on the story of its foundation, in which the Dean speaks of the "fantastic circumstances," taking us back into "a world of poetry," and of the "childish and eccentric fancies" of the Confessor, whose "opinions and prevailing motives were such as in no part of modern Europe would now be shared by any educated teacher or ruler."

The Age of Faith not the Age of Poetry.

"First, I dispute the implied statement," said Mr. Ruskin, "that the age of faith is the age of poetry. Surely the age of poetry in English history is not the age of Bede, but that of Shakespeare. The generation, too, which has seen 'Hiawatha,' and George Macdonald's 'Soul's Diary,' and Keble's Hymns might fairly claim to be an age not destitute of religious poetry. But,

to settle the matter once for all, take the following story from Bede's ' Life of Cuthbert,' which
tell how Cuthbert, on bidding some pilgrims
farewell, had bidden them also to cook a certain
goose they would find prepared for them. The
visitors finding they had enough of their own,
and to spare, went on their way, but for seven
days were detained by contrary winds, and yet
' could not think what fault they had committed.'
But when they went back to the holy father, and
he found that the goose had not been eaten, he
reproved their disobedience, and said, 'No wonder
that the storm has prevented you.' So he bade
them put the goose into the cauldron. And lo,
as soon as the kettle began to boil the wind
dropped and the waves were still! This story,
which Bede had, he tells us, ' not on chance
authority, but from a very pious and reverend
monk who was present at the time,' I give you,"
said Mr. Ruskin, "partly as an illustration of
the power of obedience, but chiefly in order
that we may hear no more about the poetry of
the age of Bede."

The Age of Faith not " Childish."

"But Dean Stanley tells us, in the second
place, that it was an ' artless and childish' age.
On the contrary, it was an age which was
eminently productive of, eminently under the
governance and guidance of, men of the widest
and most brilliant faculties, constructive and
speculative, men whose acts became the romance,

whose thoughts the wisdom, and whose arts the treasure of a thousand years of futurity." In illustration of this point Mr. Ruskin said—

"Again and again they would indeed find the stream of the Gospel contracting itself into narrow channels, and appearing, after long-concealed filtration through veins of unmeasured rock, with the bright resilience of a mountain spring. But they would find it the only candid, and therefore the only wise, way of research to look in each era of Christendom for the minds of culminating power in all its brotherhood of nations, and careless of local impulse, momentary zeal, picturesque incident, or vaunted miracle, to fasten their attention upon the force of character in the men whom over each newly converted race Heaven visibly sets forth its shepherds and kings, to bring forth judgment and victory. Of these he would name to them, as messengers of God and masters of men, five monks and five kings, in whose arms the life of the world lay as a nursling babe. Let them remember, in their successive order —of monks, St. Jerome, St. Augustine, St. Martin, St. Benedict, and St. Gregory; of kings, Theodoric, Charlemagne, Alfred, Canute, and the Confessor."

"Of three of these men," Mr. Ruskin continued, "I will read you some words which I will ask you to compare with whatever is best and most exalted in the literature of to-day. For philosophy Mr. Ruskin recited a passage from St. Augustine's 'Citie of God;' for Christian prayer, Alfred's expansion of the words, *Fiat voluntas tua;* and for Christian polity, the well-known letter which Canute sent to England from Rome, 'that all the people of my realm may rejoice in my well doing.' What think you, in candour and honour," Mr. Ruskin asked, " you youths of enlightenment, of the spirit that thus animated the dark ages? Whatever you may feel respecting the beauty and wisdom of the words I have read to you, be assured of one thing above all, that they were sincere. The idea of diplomacy or priestcraft belongs only to comparatively recent times. No false knight or lying priest ever prospered in the 'dark' ages; men succeeded only by following openly declared purposes and preaching candidly beloved and trusted creeds."

The Pleasures of Faith.

In so believing and loving they were joyous as well as sincere. "We continually hear," said Mr. Ruskin, in conclusion, "of the trials, and sometimes of the victories of faith, but scarcely ever of its pleasures. Yet the chief delight of all good men, in all the ages, has been in recognizing the goodness of the Master who had come to dwell in their spirits. In all we now do we expose ourselves to countless miseries, because we depend only on our own power, and choose only our own gratification—with no thought of working, except for ourselves or others in whose welfare we are equally selfishly interested, until the idea of acting with any other object has come to be like the precentor's invitation to a company of little voice and less practice to 'sing to the praise and glory of God.' You cannot any longer imagine the pleasures of faith, perhaps, but you can assuredly prove them. Simply as

a philosophical experiment, adopt the principles
of Alfred or Augustine for a year. If, then,
you are no happier, at least you will be able
with more grace and more modesty to be of the
same opinion still. If you are minded thus to
try, begin each day with Alfred's prayer; then
set to work with no thought of ambition, or gain,
or pleasure more than is appointed you, but
with a steady determination to do something
for the help or honour of your country, resolving not to join in the world's iniquities, nor to
turn aside from its miseries. Live thus, and
believe that with a swiftness of answer proportionate to the truth of your endeavour the
God of hope will fill you with all peace and joy.
But if you have not courage nor art enough to
make the trial, if you allow yourselves to be
hindered by the wishes of your friends, or the
interest of your families, or the bias of your
genius, or the expectations of your college, or
any other bow-wow-wow of this wild dog of a
world, then for very shame give up all title to
be free or independent, and recognize yourselves
for the slaves you are, with your thoughts put
in ward to your bodies, and your hearts bound
in manacles to your hands; then, for very
shame, if you cannot believe that there were
once men who gave their souls to God, know
and confess how surely there are those who sell
themselves to His adversaries."

Lecture III.

"The Confessor to Cœur-de-Lion: the Pleasures of Deed."

(Pall Mall Gazette, November 3rd, 1884.)

THE 3rd chapter of Mr. Ruskin's history differed from the other two in not having been completely written out when the time came for the delivery of the lecture last Saturday. The work had been interfered with, it seems, partly by a visit from a Birmingham gentleman—the trustee of St. George's Guild—and partly by a dinner with "my dear Professor Westwood," both of which events, it will be seen, suggested happy thoughts which Mr. Ruskin had not time to fully work in. So, again, the historical extracts required for the illustration of his lectures were on this occasion curtailed, because "the University insists on building ball-rooms instead of lecture-rooms, and I do not care to keep you further imprisoned in this black hole." The following abstract, however, will perhaps give a general idea of Mr. Ruskin's line of argument :—

Saxons versus *Normans.*

In his first two lectures he had given some reasons for doubting whether our Saxon ancestors were as fantastic and childish as Dean

Stanley represents them.   He now went a step
farther, and showed that there was such force
in their infancy and grace in their fantasy as
to make extremely disputable the Dean's final
statement that the Norman invasion was entirely
a sanitary, moral, and intellectual blessing to
England, and that the arrow which struck her
Harold was indeed the arrow of the Lord's
deliverance.   Was the rule of the Norman really
"the avenging, civilizing, stimulating hand of
a mightier race"? and did the future of the
Saxons indeed depend on the critical advent of
the didactic and disciplinary Norman barons
to polish them, stimulate, and chastise ?   One
thing, at least, Mr. Ruskin's audience would,
after his last lecture, be ready, perhaps, to admit,
and that was that the Saxon character, with its
imagination, its docility, its love of knowledge,
gave rise to one of the purest and most intellectual forms of faith that Christendom has ever
seen.   It has, however, never been understood
—partly because of the rudeness of its expression in the illumination of manuscripts, and its
total want of expression in architecture, but
chiefly from its own childlike character, and its
fearless application of great principles to small
things.

Norman Religion: the Gospel of Works.

Just as this faith was springing to its fruit-
age comes the Norman invasion.   How far this
was an advantage may be seen far better by

considering Alfred's struggle against the Vikings
than Harold's against William, whose Normans
had been touched by Christianity. They had
been touched, but that is all; for the first thing
to notice about the Normans is that they never
were Christians, nor ever tried to be, but only
enemies of the Saracens. For detailed knowledge about the Normans, between 800 A.D.
and 1200, Mr. Ruskin referred to the scattered
notices in M. Viollet le Duc's Dictionary of
Architecture—the best informed, most intelligent, and most thoughtful of guides—and contented himself with gathering up the general
results. One needful caution, by the way, Mr.
Ruskin interposed to his erudite critics : rough
generalizations of four centuries in so many
minutes must not be understood without exceptions or taken *au pied de la lettre*. As he read
them, these Normans were men wholly of this
world, bent on doing the most in it and making
the best of it they could—men of deeds to their
death, never pausing, changing, repenting, or
anticipating more than the completed square of
their keep and roof of their nave. In religion
they cared neither for its sentiments nor its
promises, but they adopted it solely as an instrument of order. Their attitude was thus the
exact reverse of that of the modern believer, of
whom it may be generally said that he values
religion as promising future bliss, not as enforcing present duty. The Norman searches the
Scriptures, adopts every exhortation to do and
govern, and proclaims himself blunt knight of

God—liable to much misapprehension, of course, as to the services immediately required of him, but supposing, since the whole make of him, outside and in, was a soldier, that God meant him for a soldier, and that he was to establish by main force the Christian faith and works all over the world, so far as he comprehended them ; not with the Mohammedan indignation against spiritual error, but with a sound and honest soul's dislike of material error, and resolution to extinguish that, even if perchance found in the spiritual persons to whom, in their office, he yet rendered total reverence.

Norman Art : the Rule of Strength.

So, too, in art, the Normans make no books of their churches, write no " Bibles of Amiens " on their porches.   As soon as they entered France—

" They became hardy and active builders. Within the space of a century and a half they had covered the country on which they had definitely landed with religious, monastic, and civil edifices, of an extent and richness then little common.   They set themselves to build impregnable military walls, and sublime religious ones, in the best possible practical ways.   Soldiers before and after everything, they learned the lockings and bracings of their stones primarily in defence against the battering-ram and the projectile, and esteemed the pure circular arch for its distributed and equal strength more than for its beauty."

The pictured wall belongs not to the Normans. And here came in—brought, we may suppose,

by "Fors Clavigera"—a very happy illustration,
suggested by Mr. Ruskin's Birmingham friend,
Mr. Baker.   Mr. Ruskin was showing him, only
the day before, the collection of antique casts
which Mr. W. B. Richmond had so wisely
brought to supersede "the modern stuff of
Chantrey," and on stopping under the Athena
of Ægina Mr. Baker exclaimed, "Hallo! why,
there's the chopped Norman arch!"   And there,
sure enough (Mr. Ruskin added) it was, and I
had never seen it.   The chopped Norman arch
and the fringe in which you young ladies delight
come alike from the forehead of Athena.   Nor
was this all, for on the edge of her cestus Mr.
Ruskin found the foliation which he showed in a
photograph of Poictiers, just as from her peplus
comes the drapery of Rheims.   Mr. Ruskin
gave another interesting instance of the dependence of the Normans on the art of Greece.   A
few years ago he went to Sicily to see the tombs
of Roger and of Frederick (cf. p. 85), and to
look at the Norman art he would surely find
there.   But not a stroke of the chisel turned
out to belong to the Normans.   Their own
masons could not carve, and the tombs of the
Norman kings are the work of Greek slaves.
What the Greeks carved was a lion with
the Gorgon's head—again with the chopped
Norman arch in the fringe; and what the
Normans themselves made of the Gorgon may
be seen on Iffley Church.   Mr. Ruskin here
showed an enlarged drawing of a grotesque
head—the Gorgon, with long ears, and the face

elongated by the Norman helmet—the whole effect bearing a striking resemblance to Mephistopheles, of which gentleman Mr. Ruskin promised to say more in later lectures.

The Pleasures of Deed—in War.

Both in religion, then, and in art, the pleasures of the Normans were those not of faith, but of deeds. Of these pleasures of deed Mr. Ruskin gave many illustrations from Sismondi's " Norman Conquest of Sicily," only " touching Sismondi up here and there, where he is too cool, or where he fails to see far enough into things." Mr. Ruskin referred especially to the off-hand determination of the Normans in 1041, that " as they *were* there they might as well destroy the Byzantine Empire;" to the deeds of Robert Guiscard (so politely described as " M. Guiscard" by the *Daily News*); and above all to the battle of Civitella, on Waterloo Day, 1053, describing how the handful of Normans routed the Papal forces, and then how Leo IX. met the Norman army alone, and as he approached they threw themselves on their knees, covered themselves with dust, and implored his pardon and his blessing—" a day of deeds, gentlemen, that, to some purpose, at any rate. A piece of poetry, too, if you like, but a piece of steel-clad fact also, compared to which the battles of Hastings and Waterloo were mere boys' quarrels. You do not suppose, you British boys, that you overthrew Napoleon

when your Prime Minister folded up the map of
Europe at the thought of him.   Not you, but
the snows of Heaven and the acts of Him who
dasheth in pieces with a rod of iron."

A Defence of Norman " Thieving."

Mr. Ruskin here diverged to meet an objec-
tion which he supposed the extreme probity of
the nineteenth century would feel acutely against
these men—that they all lived by thieving :—

Without venturing (said Mr. Ruskin) to allude to the
raison d'être of the present French and English Stock
Exchanges, I will merely ask any of you, whether of
Saxon or Norman blood, to define for yourselves what
you mean by the "possession of India."   I have no
doubt that you all wish to keep India in order, and in
like manner the Duke William wished to keep England
in order.   If you will read the lecture on the life of Sir
Herbert Edwardes * (not Prince Albert Edward, as the
Standard loyally had it), which I hope to give in London
after finishing this course, you will see how a Christian
British officer could, and did verily with his whole heart,
keep in order such part of India as might be entrusted
to him, and so doing secured our empire.   But the
silent feeling and practice of the nation about India are
based on quite other motives than Sir Herbert's.   Every
mutiny, every danger, every terror, and every crime
occurring under or paralyzing our Indian legislation
arises directly out of our national desire to live on the
loot of India ; and the notion of English young gentlemen and ladies of good position, falling in love with
each other without immediate prospect of establishment
in Belgrave Square, that they can find in India, instantly
on landing, a bungalow ready furnished with the loveliest

* See "A Knight's Faith," vol. iv. of "Bibliotheca
Pastorum" (George Allen, 1885).

fans, china, and shawls, ices and sherbet at command, four-and-twenty slaves succeeding each other hourly to swing the punkah, and a regiment with a beautiful band to "keep order" outside, all round the house.

The Old Lion and the New.

Mr. Ruskin's peroration had not got itself written on Saturday afternoon, but the scornful moral with which his lectures are wont to conclude was pointed very effectively by some pictures instead. The first illustration was the lucky outcome of his dinner with Professor Westwood, who had shown him the Bible of Charles the Bald, the tutor of Alfred. The illuminated frontispiece which Mr. Ruskin showed is the figure of a true lion, inscribed beneath with words which run, being interpreted, "This lion rises, and by his rising breaks the gates of hell. This lion never sleeps, nor shall sleep for evermore." Such was the lion as our Saxon Alfred knew it. For Richard Cœur de Lion Mr. Ruskin referred his audience to "Fors Clavigera" (No. III., March, 1871) and the later chapters of "Ivanhoe." "Men called him 'Lion-heart,' not untruly; and the English as a people have prided themselves somewhat ever since on having every man of them the heart of a lion. Many lion-hearted Englishmen there have been, and are indeed still to this day; but for the especial peculiar typical product of the nineteenth century see this page of *Punch*." Mr. Ruskin here displayed in a frame the inside fold of *Punch* for August 16th, 1884, containing

Q

on the left-hand page a drawing, by Mr. Du
Maurier, of the different effects of a good
dinner on two fat old gentlemen, and on the
right a cartoon of Mr. Bright as "The Old
Lion Aroused." Mr. Ruskin had inserted a
connecting mark between the two pictures,
and christened the whole

" *The New Lion Stuffed.*"

Lecture IV.

"Cœur de Lion to Elizabeth :
the Pleasures of Fancy."

(*Pall Mall Gazette*, November 10th, 1884.)

Mr. Ruskin's History has been "shoved all
wrong," as he told his audience on Saturday,
by the lucky accidents which he described in
his last lecture. The fourth lecture had to fill
up some of the gaps in the third, and the result
is that the History is getting a good deal behind
date. No one need complain, however, since
the result is that Mr. Ruskin has now promised
some further lectures to supplement the present
course, as well as a special one on Giorgione,
with a description of whose altar-piece at Castel Franco Saturday's miscellany was, as will
be seen lower down, brought to an eloquent
conclusion.

" *The Five Christmas Days.*"

The first gap in his last lecture which Mr. Ruskin filled up on Saturday was an enumeration of the " Five Christmas Days " which, as it happens, sum up the history of five centuries. These dates were written down on a diagram which hung conspicuously on the wall behind the lecturer, and are as follows: Christmas Day 496, Clovis baptized; 800, Charlemagne crowned; 1041, the Vow of the Count of Aversa (the settlement of the Normans, near Naples, whose vow was referred to in the last lecture); 1066, the Conqueror crowned; 1130, Roger II. crowned King of the Two Sicilies. These Christmas Days will be referred to in later lectures, said Mr. Ruskin, in connection with the way in which you keep Christmas Days now.

An Ideal Election.

The filling up of another gap was also a correction. In the last lecture I gave you incidentally (said Mr. Ruskin) what was, in my opinion, extremely good advice—namely, never to make a shot at anything, neither at a word —no, nor at a bird. I was the better qualified to give that sage advice because I was at the moment making a shot myself at the name of the Venetian Doge who was defeated by Robert Guiscard. I thought at the time it was Pietro Orseolo, but I now remember that it was

Domenico Selvo. Taking this slip apparently as an accident sent by "Fors," Mr. Ruskin proceeded to say some more about this great Doge, reading from the chapter entitled "Divine Right," in "St. Mark's Rest"—a chapter which was always meant, Mr. Ruskin said, for a lecture, since much of its meaning depended on accent. It describes how the people of Venice went in armed boats to the Lido, and prayed that " God would grant to them such a king as should be worthy to reign over them ; " and how suddenly, as they prayed, there rose up with one accord among the multitude the cry, " Domenico Selvo, we will, and we approve." Carlyle has given you a description of a grand election in that of the Abbot Samson, but this is a grander still. The chapter then goes on to tell how Domenico entered barefoot the Field of St. Mark (all covered with green grass then), how he gave the people pillage of his palace ("modern bribery is quite as costly and not half so merry"), and how he afterwards took a Greek maid for his wife, whose luxury, especially in the use of "certain two-pronged instruments" wherewith to eat her meat, was miraculous in the eyes of simple Venice, but whose reign "first gave the glories of Venetian art, in true inheritance from the angels, of that Athenian Rock above which Ion spread his starry tapestry, and under whose shadow his mother had gathered the crocus in the dew."

A Digression.

The mention of " Ion " led Mr. Ruskin into a little digression about the violet, for Euripides' violet was the *viola odorata* of pure blue, the *fleur-de-lis* of Byzantine ornament. Gathering it at its home at Palermo long ago, said Mr. Ruskin, I matched it against the "violet sea," and could not tell which was which. Here are my drawings of the sea and of the flower. I have given you in the Turner gallery, here in Oxford, his rendering of the Mediterranean Sea —more skilful in its effect of haze than mine, but mine, I think, a little more true in colour; at any rate I put all the colour in my box on it. It is a picture of what spring grass is like—in Sicily you cannot say whether it is green or blue, pure white in Florence and in France, and gold here on Isis' banks, till your horrible races came and embanked the stream, and the noisy crowds of you trampled the flowers.

" Imagination" and " Fancy."

Returning now "to business," Mr. Ruskin gave a preliminary definition of what he meant by imagination. " In ' Modern Painters ' I distinguished unnecessarily between fancy and imagination. Dean Stanley's word 'fantasy' is accurate for both, fancy being concerned with lighter things. When a boy falls foolishly in love with a girl you say he has taken a fancy

for her; but if he loves her rightly, that is to
say for her noble qualities, you ought to say he
has taken an imagination for her; for then he
is endowed with the new light of love, which
sees and tells of the mind in her. And not
falsely or vainly. Wordsworth, indeed, says of
his wife, most foolishly and conceitedly—

> 'Such if thou wert in all men's view,
>   An universal show,
> What would my fancy have to do,
>   My feelings to bestow?'

thus making of her a mere lay figure for the
drapery of his fancy. But the true lover's love
discovers, not bestows—discovers what is most
precious in his mistress, and what works most
deeply for his life and happiness. Day by day,
as he loves her better, he discerns her more
truly."

"*Imagination*" and "*Truth.*"

"The truth and faith of the lover are the
foundation of all the joy in imagination, that is
to say in truths of configuration. When in my
next lecture I speak of the pleasures of truth I
mean untransfigured truth, whereas what the
imagination exercises itself upon is configured
truth. Thus, you may look at a girl until she
seems to you an angel, because, at best, all girls
are angels; but no amount of looking at a cock-
chafer will convert it into a girl. The conse-
quences of the frank and eager use of the fancy

on religious subjects are to be seen in the
change from the 'three whales' cubs' to the
perfect types of the Virgin and Son—Divine,
because, with most affectionate truth, human.
This apotheosis by the imagination is the subject of the present lecture: to-day I only describe it; in the next lecture I shall discuss it."

Mythic and Real Saints.

An important distinction is to be noted in
the objects of this apotheosis, according as they
are, or are not, real persons. The first class includes the mythic saints, who are often merely
revived Pagan deities; the second includes
men and women who really lived, but whose
memories are illumined by tradition. The
mythic saints belong chiefly to the southern
races; the Goths have their saints of flesh and
blood, and in all the art by Loire and Seine you
will never find either river personified. The
ideal Charity of Giotto at Padua tramples upon
bags of gold, gives only corn and flowers, while
God's angel gives her, not even these, but a
heart. The Charity on the west porch of
Amiens clothes a beggar with the staple manufacture of the town. Under the former exercise
of the imagination the lion personifies the
Evangelists; an angel, justice; and some personification is found for every Platonic myth
and Athanasian article.

The Glorious Company of Saints.

Mr. Ruskin then went through some of the
saints, whose glorious company was one of
the pleasures of imagination—speaking first of
St. Sophia, the pacific and scholastic ghost of
Athena; and of St. Catherine of Egypt, of whom
there are some vestiges of personality, and who
may possibly have existed.   However that may
be—witty, proud, fanciful—she is the bride in
Solomon's Song, combining the purest life of
the nun with the brightest death of a martyr.
St. Barbara of Egypt—confined, like Danæ, in
a tower (*inclusam Danaën turris aënea*)—is of
all saints the most practical, the personification
of the art of building; not a pillar in Giotto's
Santa Maria del Fiore, as Mr. Ruskin says of
her in " Ethics of the Dust," which Athena did
not set true by her spear-shaft as it rose; and
her tower is the perfected symbol of Gothic
architecture.   She is protectress against light-
ning, and the first to hear the petition in the
Litany against sudden death.   The later legends,
connecting her with cannon and gunpower—
with attack instead of defence—are a base corruption; and no doubt we shall have her next
as the figure-head of an ironclad.   St. Margaret
of Antioch—the Geneviève of the East, winning
a soul's victory like Alcestis—is the type of all
meekness and gentleness, the pattern of all
gracious and lowly womanhood.   Of St. Cecilia
I may say—like the carter in Miss Edgeworth's

"Harry and Lucy," who refuses to believe the story of the upset till he hears the name of the hill where it took place—that a visit to her Church in Rome establishes the legend of her. She is of course the patron saint of music, but her true note is not so often insisted upon. In a manuscript dated 1290, in Mr. Ruskin's possession—"I have selfishly kept it in my own house, but it shall go to your schools now"—there is this story of St. Cecilia told: While the organs were playing Cecilia sang to the Lord, that He would keep her heart in purity. "We have hardly so clear a notion of the baptizing, purifying power of music now, and St. Cecilia's presence at a Monday Pop would be as little expected as desired." Of all the mythic saints she is the greatest, and all who strive to purify themselves by fireside or wayside may hear Cecilia sing. For St. Ursula Mr. Ruskin referred to "Fors Clavigera;" and of the second class of saints who really lived, he only enumerated, taking their French names from St. Louis's Psalter, Magdalen, Geneviève, Scholastica, Agatha, Felicitas, Christina, Honorine, Euphemia, Eugenia. Of Magdalen alone Mr. Ruskin made one remark, that any woman, whatever her position, who sells herself for money is a harlot, while Magdalen is the type of those for whom the guilt of others around them have "taken away my Christ; I know not where they have laid Him."

Figures of the Saints.

Mr. Ruskin then passed to a second pleasure of imagination—not any longer that of exalting the memory of dead persons, but that of setting up their images and investing them with sanctity. "Fors Clavigera" came in the form of a letter from Miss Alexander ("Francesca") to clench this matter with an illustration from modern Italian life. In this letter Miss Alexander describes the Madonna whom she saw enshrined in an orphanage as a stout heavy person in impossible drapery—much improved of late in cleanliness, if not in beauty or sanctity, by a coating of white oil paint. One of the girls had given her a rose, another a set of earrings. "I pierced the ears myself," added the Lady Superior, "with a gimlet." There, said Mr. Ruskin, you have the perfection of childlike imagination—making everything out of nothing.*

Giorgione and Tintoret.

Of Saturday's lecture a written peroration was again wanting, and the conclusion of the whole matter was shown instead in two pictures

* The letter from Francesca referred to above will be found in ch. 3 of vol. i. of "Christ's Folk in the Apennine" (George Allen, 1887), where Mr. Ruskin says of the Madonna story, "There is no passage in all these histories which claims from the general reader more tender and loving attention, or in reading which he ought to repent more solemnly of light thought and scornful mood, or to remember with more shame the iconoclasm of Churches that had neither sense nor charity."

—" the two most perfect pictures in the world."
One was a small piece from Tintoret's Paradise
in the Ducal Palace, representing the group
of St. Ambrose, St. Jerome, St. Gregory, St.
Augustine, and behind St. Augustine "his
mother watching him, her chief joy in Paradise."
There was some little movement of laughter
among the audience as Mr. Ruskin found that
he had placed the sketch upside down. But it
is little matter, he added, for in Tintoret's Paradise you have heaven all round you—a work of
pure imagination, and that, too, by a dyer's son
in Venice. The other picture was the Arundel
Society's reproduction ("a Society which has
done more for us than we have any notion of")
of the altar-piece by Giorgione, in his native
hamlet of Castel Franco. "No picture in the
world can show you better the seeing and realizing imagination of Christian painters. Giorgione in no wise intends you to suppose that
the Madonna ever sat thus on a pedestal with
a coat of arms upon it, or that St. George and
St. Francis ever stood, or do now stand, in that
manner beside her; but that a living Venetian
may, in such vision, most deeply and rightly
conceive of her and of them. As such this
picture is alone in the world, as an imaginative
representation of Christianity, with a monk and
a soldier on either side, the soldier bearing the
white cross of everlasting peace on the purple
ground of former darkness."

It would appear (said the *Pall Mall Gazette,*

by way of supplement to the above report), from
one of the incidental passages of autobiography
in Mr. Ruskin's lecture on Saturday, that he is
as much a victim of the demon of noise as
was his master Carlyle. Among other passages
which he read was one from Carlyle's "Frederick the Great," in which it is told how Adalbert,
Bishop of Prague, was sleeping by the roadside
when "a Bohemian shepherd chanced to pass
that way, warbling something on his pipe,
as he wended towards looking after his flock;
and seeing the sleeper on his stone pillow, the
thoughtless Czech mischievously blew louder."
Adalbert awoke, and shrieked in his fury,
"Deafness on thee, man cruel to the human
sense of hearing!"—or words to that effect.
The curse was punctually fulfilled, and the
fellow was deaf for the rest of his life. What
a pity, said Mr. Ruskin, that you have no Bishop
Adalbert in Oxford! You think yourselves very
musical, with your twiddlings and fiddlings of
organs after service, but you allow "that beastly
hooter" to wake me every morning, and so to
make life among you intolerable in these days.

Lecture V.

"Protestantism: the Pleasures of Truth."

(*Pall Mall Gazette*, November 17th, 1884.)

THE space in the history of Christianity covered
by the present lecture cannot, Mr. Ruskin began

by saying on Saturday, be defined by the reigns
of any particular kings or queens, because the
movement with which it is concerned takes
place at different times, in different countries.
He could only define it, therefore, by its character, calling it the period of Protestantism,
including the two movements known severally
in history as the Reformation and the Revolution.

The Reformation and the Revolution.

Every country passes through one Reformation and one Revolution—reformation, when it
bears witness for spiritual truth against manifest
falsehood; revolution, when it secures the rights
of the subjects from tyranny. Of the Reformation in all countries and times, John Knox
is the perfect symbol ("or, if you will, Luther;
but I like Knox better"); and of the Revolution,
John Hampden—the former saying, "I won't
be cheated in religion;" the latter, "I won't be
taxed in my pockets." "Sometimes, indeed, the
Protestant fights against untruth and taxation
together, and then you have the Protestant
squire; just as sometimes the Catholic fights for
lies and taxes together, and then you have the
Catholic squire. In Scott the representatives
of the two kinds of Protestantism are Jeanie
Deans of the first, and Major Bridgenorth, in
'Peveril of the Peak,' of the other. I refer to
Scott," said Mr. Ruskin, "now and always, for
historical illustration, because he is far and

away the best writer of history we have. Our
only historians (ordinarily so called) are Carlyle,
Froude, and Helps, but none of them can see
all round a thing as Scott does. Froude does
not even know whether he is a Catholic or a
Protestant; Carlyle is first the one, and then
the other; while Helps is deficient because he
never understands Catholicism at all."

The Beauty of Protestantism.

Protestantism (continued Mr. Ruskin) is still
in the ascendant, but we Catholics think that
the day will yet come when we shall again see
visions of things that are not as though they
were, and even be able, like Edward the Confessor, to tax the people in a tenth of their
possessions to build a beautiful church with a
weathercock upon it, to rise above the filth of
nasty London. All the beauty of Protestantism
is embodied in two great masters—Scott for
English literature, Gotthelf for Continental (not
Goethe, as the *Standard* had it)—in Scott, in
the character of Jeanie Deans; in Gotthelf, in
" Ulric, the Farm Servant." The latter story,
which Mr. Ruskin said some time ago he meant
to add to " Bibliotheca Pastorum," his series
of classical books for the St. George's Library,
has been translated from the German by one
of his " best lady pupils," and was published
recently. Nothing can be more perfect or complete, Mr. Ruskin said, as a representation of
the good side of Protestantism.

The Beauty of Catholicism—in Turner.

Leaving the beauty of Protestantism, the pleasures of truth, to the description of them in these two novels, Mr. Ruskin himself turned to the other side of the question, and proposed to show rather the narrowness of its rigid truth in comparison with the beauty of the spectral phenomena in which Catholicism delights. For this purpose he had brought with him two pictures—one by Turner, the other a copy from Carpaccio. The Turner was a large water-colour drawing, measuring somewhere about 20 inches by 15 inches, in his early or brown period, of a stream and a grove. "There," said Mr. Ruskin, pointing to it, "is a spectral grove for you, the very εἴδωλον of a grove. There never was such a grove or such a stream. You may photograph every grove in the world, and never will you get so ghostly a one as this. I cannot tell you where it is; I can only swear to you that it never existed anywhere except in Turner's head. It is the very best Turner drawing I ever saw of his heroic period, the period in which he painted the 'Garden of the Hesperides' (Nat. Gall., No. 477—exhibited 1806) and 'Apollo Killing the Python' (No. 488—exhibited 1811). I picked it up by pure chance, the other day, in the shop of my friend Mr. Sewening, of Duke Street, St. James's, to whose excellent judgment, by the way, I now refer any pictures which are sent to me to verify. He thought it might be a Turner, and asked me £40 for it. I was sure it was, and gave him 50 guineas, and I now present it to your gallery at Oxford, to be an idol to you, I hope, for evermore."

In Carpaccio's " St. Ursula."

"And here," added Mr. Ruskin, turning to the other picture, "is an idol of a girl." This was a copy of the head in Carpaccio's " Dream of St. Ursula," the picture of which Mr. Ruskin has written so much in "Fors Clavigera" and his Venetian guide-books, and which was largely referred to, by the way, by Mr. Wingfield, in the recent revival of " Romeo and Juliet" at the Lyceum, for the details of a Venetian interior :—

"There never was such a face as hers in the world. Take the sweetest you can find in your college gardens, and none will be so sweet. Nor in any Phyllis that you know will you find such twisted hair as hers—twisted, like that of all Venetian girls, in memory of the time when they first made their hair into ropes for the fugitive ships at Aquileia. You will never see such hair, nor such peace beneath it on the brow—the peace of heaven, of infancy, and of death. No one knows who she is or where she lived. She is Persephone at rest below the earth ; she is Proserpine at play above the ground. She is Ursula, the gentlest yet the rudest of little bears ; a type in that, perhaps, of the moss rose, or of the rose *spinosissima*, with its rough little buds. She is in England, in Cologne, in Venice, in Rome, in eternity, living everywhere, dying everywhere, the most intangible yet the most practical of all saints, queen, for one thing, of female education, when once her legend is rightly understood. This sketch of her head is the best drawing I ever made. Carpaccio's picture is hung, like all good pictures, out of sight, seven feet above the ground; but the Venetian Academy had it taken down for me, and I traced every detail in it accurately to a hair's breadth. It took me a day's hard work to get that spray of silver hair loosening itself rightly from the coil, and twelve times over had I to try the mouth. And to-day, assuming Miss Shaw Lefevre's indulgence, I present it to the girls of Somerville Hall. Perhaps the picture of a princess's room, of which it is a part, may teach the young ladies there not to make their rooms too pretty—to remember that they come to Oxford to be uncomfortable and to suffer a little—to learn whatever can be learnt in Oxford, which is not much, and even to live as little Ursulas, in rough gardens, not on lawns made smooth for tennis."

The Wooden Walls of England.

Such is the lesson of the legend of St. Ursula; and now (continued Mr. Ruskin), I must tell you somewhat of a Doge of Venice who lived by the light of superstitions such as this, a Catholic and a brave man withal, *Cattolico uomo e audace*, "the servant of God and of St. Michael." To avoid mistakes to-day and corrections to-morrow, Mr. Ruskin craved permission to read again from his Venetian handbook, "St. Mark's Rest," which had always been meant for reading, and had now been retouched.

The longest of these new touches was suggested by "The Truth about the Navy," which Mr. Ruskin had been reading, he said, in the *Pall Mall Gazette;* from which he gathered that the British people having spent several

R

hundreds of millions on blowing iron bubbles—
"the earth hath bubbles, as the water has, and
these are of them"—would soon be busy blowing
more. Nothing could be more tragically absurd
than the loss of the *Captain* and the *London*,
unless it were the loss of the *Eurydice*—without
her Orpheus then. There was nothing the
matter, except that Governments were donkeys
enough to build in iron instead of wood, just in
order that the ironmongers might get their com-
missions. They were honest enough, these
Governments, but they allowed the ironmongers
to work them round like screws. Whoever
heard of a Venetian man-of-war going over?
A gale was nothing at all to a wooden ship;
Venice would have laughed at it, rejoiced in it.
They never heard of a Venetian being upset or
making for the shore. Why? Because they
had been broken in to the life of the rough sea.
"You think that you know what boating is;
but why don't you practise in the open sea, as
the Venetians did, instead of spoiling the Isis,
here?" But with the *London*, she was crossing
the Bay of Biscay when it got a little rough;
the wind blew the bulwarks down, and down
the ship went bodily. The only grand thing
connected with it was that the captain, looking
over the bulwarks as the last boat was launched,
gave the crew their latitude, and said he would
go down with his ship, and he did. Mr. Ruskin
had no patience, in face of disasters like those
of the *London* and the *Captain*, with all the talk
about our splendid British seamanship. It was

bombastic English blarney—not Irish, for there
was always wit in an Irish bull, but only a
double blunder in an English one—all that talk
about sweeping the fleets of all other nations off
the seas. "You went under Napier and knocked
your heads against Cronstadt, and Cronstadt
cared no more for you than if you had been a
flight of swallows or sparrows. Then you went
and knocked your heads against Sebastopol ;
and, in spite of all the lies in the newspapers,
every one knew that the British fleet had been
thoroughly well licked. And now you have
been bombarding Alexandria, and narrowly
escaped being done for by a few Arabs. So
much for the proud supremacy of the British
navy and its ironclads."* They might say that
all this was irrelevant ; but there was no finer art

* "Mr. Ruskin" (wrote the *Pall Mall Gazette*), "like the
rest of the world, is fully alive (as will be seen from the
report of his lecture in another column) to the Truth about
the Navy, and to the loss of our vaunted supremacy on the
sea. We can hardly agree with him, however, that everything would again be right if we only got rid of the
'ironmongers' and their 'bubbles,' and sent the mariners
of England to meet the Navies of the world in row-boats.
As for Mr. Ruskin's version of the truth about Protestantism, which was the main subject of his lecture, it will
be interesting to see what the *Rock*, say, will make of it.
The Catholic community in Oxford must apparently have
been forewarned of Mr. Ruskin's conversion to their party,
for there was an important deputation of them in the front
seats on Saturday afternoon, and very pretty it was to see
them cheering the winged words of their fiery ally. Every
one who knows Mr. Ruskin's earlier works will remember
how he was brought up by the strictest sect of Protestant
Evangelicalism. In his old age he ought to serve as a terrible example to Protestant mothers."

than ship-building, and they would find that out
when he set them to draw ships; they were
only drawing shells now.   Even a draughtsman
could not draw two sides of a ship alike; nobody but Turner ever did.   They might say one
of the subjects forbidden to him was political
economy; but that subject, too, would be forced
on them all pretty soon.   For when all the present ships were destroyed the new ones would
also go "snap" in like fashion.

The Nelson of Venice: a Catholic and Brave Man.

The chapter from which Mr. Ruskin was
reading when this parenthesis came in is the
one entitled "The Burden of Tyre," and tells
the story of Domenico Michiel, the Nelson of
Venice, the doge who brought back in 1126,
from his wars against the Saracens, the famous
pillars of the Piazzetta.   Besides them, he
brought the dead bodies of St. Donato and St.
Isidore; for the Venice of his day was intensely
covetous, not only of money, though she loved
that too, nor of kingdom, nor of pillars of marble
and granite, but "also and quite principally of
the relics of good people, of their dust to dust,
ashes to ashes."   He himself lies buried behind
the altar of the church of S. Giorgio Maggiore,
and on his tomb there was this inscription
written, "Whoever thou art, who cometh to
behold this tomb of his, bow thyself down
before God because of him."

Two Types of Protestant Witness.

That (said Mr. Ruskin) is the feeling of all "Old Catholics" in the presence of a shrine; they worship not the hero or the saint, but "God because of him." Against all this comes the witness of Protestantism, partly honest, partly hypocritical, with good knowledge of a few minor things, but ignorant hatred of all above and beyond itself. Here I have for you a type of the honest but not liberally minded Protestant (said Mr. Ruskin), disclosing a sketch of a little porker. The little pig walks along, you see, knowing every inch of its ground, having in its snout a capital instrument for grubbing up things. You may be shocked, perhaps, at my selection of this animal for the type of a religious sect; but if you could but realize all the beautiful things which the insolence of Protestantism has destroyed, you would think surely the Gadarene swine too good for it. But my illustration is, at any rate, appropriate as significant of the Protestant and Evangelical art which can draw a pig to perfection, but never a pretty lady. Mr. Ruskin then passed on to the hypocritical Protestant, and produced as the type of him a sketch in black and white of a truly repulsive Mr. Stiggins with a concertina.

The Heroic Ideal.

These two sketches were to illustrate the religious ghostly ideal. The heroic ideal was

illustrated from poetry. The faith in human
honour, taking the place of the faith in religion,
which is the groundwork of this ideal, passes
into the noble pride of the true knight; and it
is when this noble pride passes into malignant
pride that the Revolution comes. Of the true
knight, the perfect type is Douglas in the " Lady
of the Lake." " No one reads Scott now (Mr.
Ruskin here parenthetically remarked), and I am
going to send his poems and novels by the gross
to classes in our elementary schools—not for
prizes to be awarded by competition, but to be
given to any boy or girl who is good and likes
to read poetry. I should like to see the children
draw lots for the books, and the one who wins
not keep the book, but have the right of giving
it away—a very subtle little moral lesson."
Mr. Ruskin then read some stanzas from the
fifth canto of " The Lady of the Lake," describing the burghers' sports before King James at
Stirling, the classical passage in Scott corresponding to the games in Virgil. The passage
is typical, too, of that association with his dog,
his horse, and his falcon which is a mark of
the knight, the clown being one who cannot
keep these animals, or does not know how to
use them. It was very bad of Douglas, you
may think, to knock a man down for the sake
of a dog—a creature that we should think
nothing of torturing nowadays for a month to
find out the cause of a pimple on our own
red noses. Mr. Ruskin then went on to the
stanzas which he wished all who cared to

please him at once to learn by heart, the stanzas in which

> ' With grief the noble Douglas saw
> The commons rise against the law ; "

and bade them hear

> " Ere yet for me
> Ye break the bands of fealty."

[The remaining lectures of this course on " The Pleasures of England " were not delivered, for reasons explained at the beginning of the next Appendix.]

APPENDIX III.

A LECTURE ON "PATIENCE."

(*Pall Mall Gazette*, November 24th, 1884.)

No better proof can be given of Mr. Ruskin's popularity at Oxford than the fact that he played off a practical joke on the five hundred people who crowded the Museum theatre to hear him on Saturday afternoon, and yet aroused no perceptible resentment. They had all come—an hour before the time, too, many of them—to hear the sixth of his appointed course of lectures on the "Pleasures of England;" but he straightway announced that this lecture would be postponed till Monday week, and meanwhile he proposed to read them a little essay on Patience. The innocent joke, it should at once be said, was not altogether of Mr. Ruskin's own devising. The remaining lectures of the proper course were ready, but pressure had been brought to bear upon him to suppress or recast them. The details of these lectures had so far "fluttered the dovecots of the vivisectionists" that there had even been threats of the intervention of a Board of Studies, and of the

264

incarceration of their single-handed antagonist.*
Why they were so much afraid of his discussing
the pleasures of sense he really could not think.
All the beautiful things he had showed them in
religious art appealed to the pleasure of sense.
Every religious child is happy; and all religion,
if it is true, is beautiful; it is only sham religion
—the habit, for instance, of excessive mourning
for the dead—and vice that are ugly. When
they heard the lecture they would see that he
was only going to point out to them some new
and innocent ways of enjoying themselves.

The unkind critics who had caused all this
confusion were—so it was said in Oxford—Mr.
Macdonald and Dr. Acland. Mr. Ruskin had
taken their rebuke meekly; but if it was on
behalf of science that Dr. Acland was afraid,
Mr. Ruskin clearly means to have his revenge.
For in the meanwhile he promised to give a
scientific lecture (see Appendix IV.); and Mr.
Ruskin's scientific lectures do not greatly please
the recognized professors of science. "I shall
not tell you," Mr. Ruskin said, "how long a
bird's larynx is, for I don't know and I don't

---

* Writing from Oxford on December 1st, 1884, to Miss
Beever, Mr. Ruskin said, "I gave my fourteenth, and last
for this year, lecture this afternoon, with vigour and effect
(*i.e.* the Lecture on Birds, Appendix IV.), and am safe and
well (D.G.) after such a spell of work as I never did before.
I have been thrown a week out in all my plans, by having
to write two new lectures, instead of those the University
was frightened at. The scientists slink out of my way
now, as if I were a mad dog, for I let them have it hot
and hearty whenever I've a chance at them" ("Hortus
Inclusus," p. 87).

care, but I can tell you something about its singing. I can tell you about its feathers, but not
what is underneath its skin. Why, I went into
your museum to find an Abyssinian kingfisher
—the classical halcyon—but there was only one,
hidden in a dark corner, and that not a good
enough specimen to draw. A very sad thing
that, and even sadder that they should pack
away the skins of the birds in drawers in ' stink-
ing camphor.' In the British Museum, however,
you can now for the first time see birds poised,
and how they fly. I told Dr. Günther,* the
Keeper of Zoology (in the second chapter of
' Love's Meinie,' for example), and he's now
telling you." Next Saturday, Mr. Ruskin added,
I shall do a little more " peacocking " before
you, and am going to show you some practical
experiments—with the help of the Balliol College
cook—of glaciers and glacier motion. Here,

---

* Referring to the above report, Mr. Ruskin wrote to the
Pall Mall Gazette as follows : 84, Woodstock Road, Oxford,
November 25th.—Sir,—Again thanking you for the general
care and fulness of your reports, permit me to correct the
sentence referring to the head of the Zoological Department
in the British Museum, as it is given in your account of my
lecture on Saturday. I said that in ' Love's Meinie ' I had for
the first time explained to my Oxford pupils how birds flew,
and that now Dr. Günther had beautifully *shown* the birds
of England to us all, in the perfect action of flying. But I
never said I had 'told Dr. Günther' anything. Everything
he has so beautifully done has been his own bettering of
what had been begun by Mr. Gould ; it fulfils, or supersedes,
much of what I meant to attempt at Sheffield, and leaves
me, I am thankful to say, more free to my proper work
here. Dr. Günther continually tells *me* things, in all sorts
of kind ways, but I never told, or *could* have told, him anything.—I am, Sir, your obedient servant, J. Ruskin."

again, Mr. Ruskin has an old quarrel, as every one knows, with the men of science.

The prospect of these two dainty dishes should itself have made the lesson of patience easier. As Mr. Ruskin told the girls in the "Ethics of the Dust," there was obviously no reason why his audience, because they were the richer by the expectation of playing at a new game—of having two new lectures thrown in—should make themselves unhappier than when they had nothing to look forward to but the old ones. And then, even when the little lecture itself began, Mr. Ruskin often stopped from his reading to throw sugar-plums to his pupils, Were there any of them courting, for instance? Then his advice was to continue it as long as possible. "Young people nowadays do not enjoy their courtship half enough; it really becomes nicer and nicer the longer it lasts. Besides, you are all sure to find fault with your wives when you marry them; it is only during courtship that they are entirely faultless and seraphic; and why not keep them so as long as you can?" Then there was a little critical squib, *apropos* of a citation of Keats's phrase, "human serpentry." "Read as much Keats as possible, and no Shelley. Shelley, with due admiration, notwithstanding, for his genius, is entirely mischievous, Keats entirely innocent and amusing." As for the little essay on Patience itself, it consisted of readings, with occasional self-criticism, from the "Cestus of Aglaia" and "St. Mark's Rest." The "Cestus

of Aglaia" was the title given to the papers
which Mr. Ruskin contributed to the *Art Journal* in 1856–7, on "The Opposition of Modesty
and Liberty, and the Unescapable Law of Wise
Restraint," and some of which were afterwards
incorporated in "The Queen of the Air." Were
they the passages in that book, one wonders,
which Carlyle told Mr. Froude, "went into
his heart like arrows"? The passage read
on Saturday, however, was none of these
chapters, but was the analysis of Chaucer's
"Patience:"—

> "Dame Patientia sitting there I fond,
> With facë pale, upon a hill of sond."

Mr. Ruskin apologized for the over-allusive
style in which much of this analysis was written,
for "twenty years ago I was always fond of
showing that I knew a good deal and had read
a good deal." Elsewhere, too, he has explained,
with reference to these same chapters in the *Art
Journal*, that he has "three different ways of
writing—one, with the single view of making
myself understood, in which I necessarily omit
a good deal of what comes into my head;
another, in which I say what I think ought to
be said, in what I suppose to be the best words
I can find for it (which is in reality an affected
style); and my third way of writing is to say
all that comes into my head for my own pleasure, in the first words that come, retouching
them afterwards into (approximate) grammar."
The "Cestus of Aglaia" was written in this

third style. From the Patience of Chaucer,
Mr. Ruskin passed to the Patience of Venice.
The Patience who really smiles at grief usually
stands, or walks, or even runs. She seldom
sits, though she may sometimes have to do it for
many a day, poor thing, by monuments, or like
Chaucer's, with "facë pale, upon a hill of sond."
The Patience of Venice is to be found on a
monument—the statue of St. Theodore, whose
legend Mr. Ruskin has explained in "Fors
Clavigera" (March, 1877), and again in the 2nd
chapter of "St. Mark's Rest," from which he
read on Saturday. In these later books of his,
when he talks in what Mr. Matthew Arnold
calls his "assured way" about the meaning of
legends, he is only collating the results of a
life's work, begun when he was twenty-four
years old, and when, by the good counsel of
Dean Liddell, he took to drawing religious art in
the Christ Church library. All early religious
art is symbolic, and the meaning of the symbols
is well ascertainable. The divinity of Botticelli, for instance, is a science at least as well
known as that of the Greek gods, and all Mr.
Ruskin does is to give the result of the Catholic
knowledge of the saints—the interpretation
which is universally recognized of their legends.
St. Theodore, then, standing on a crocodile, as
he may be seen on one of the twin pillars of
the Piazzetta at Venice, represents the power
of the Spirit of God in all noble and useful
animal life, conquering what is venomous, useless, or in decay. The victory of his Patience is

making the earth his pedestal instead of his adversary; he is the power of gentle and rational life, reigning over the wild creatures and senseless forces of the world—the dragon-enemy becoming by human mercy the faithfullest of creature friends to man.

Besides the essay on Patience, Mr. Ruskin set to work on Saturday on a clearing-up and putting right of the "heterogeneous rubble" which some of the newspapers had made of his remarks on the British Navy last week. With a pretty compliment to his pupils, he asked them to sympathize with the bewilderment of the paltry British press in its attempt to reduce to the level of British press understanding lectures which were prepared only for their higher intelligence. Mr. Ruskin then repeated what he had before said about the loss of the *London*, the *Captain*, and the *Eurydice*. To these disasters he now added a much antecedent one—that of the *Royal George*, which was sunk in the harbour, with most of her crew, while the captain was writing in the cabin, because a few of them were hunting rats half a minute too long in her hull. They had thus four accurate illustrations of a kind of shipbuilding and ship management of which there was no parallel whatever, either among the Saxons, Vikings, Venetians, Carthaginians, Athenians, or Normans. These catastrophes belonged exclusively to modern naval history, which had its triumphs, but was darkened by many more shadows than the features which beautified it. As for the remedy, Mr. Ruskin has explained long ago, in " Fors," the incompatibility of seamanship with iron. "You need not think," he said, "that you can ever have seamen in iron ships ; it is not in flesh and blood to be vigilant when vigilance is so slightly necessary; the best seaman born will lose his qualities when he knows he can steam against wind and tide, and has to handle ships so large that the care of them is necessarily divided among many persons. If you want sea captains indeed, like Sir Richard Grenville or Lord Dundonald, you must give them small ships and wooden ones—nothing but oak, pine, and hemp to trust to, above or below—and those trustworthy."

APPENDIX IV.

"Birds, and How to Paint Them."

(*Pall Mall Gazette*, December 3rd, 1884. For the preparation of this report Mr. Ruskin lent me his own manuscript notes.)

Town and Country Life.

" I HAVE scarcely any heart to address you to-day," Mr. Ruskin began by saying on Saturday, " so terrified am I, and so subdued, by the changes in Oxford which have taken place even since first I accepted this Professorship, and which are directly calculated to paralyze all my efforts to be useful in it. I need scarcely tell any of my pupils that my own Art teaching has been exclusively founded on the hope of getting people to enjoy country life, and to care for its simple pleasures and modest employments. But I find now that the ideal in the minds of all young people, however amiable and well-meaning, is to marry as soon as possible, and then to live in the most fashionable part of the largest town they can afford to compete with the rich inhabitants of, in the largest house they can strain their incomes to the rent of, with the water laid on at the top, the gas at the bottom, huge plate-glass windows, out of which they may look uninterruptedly at a brick wall, a drawing-room on the scale of Buckingham Palace, with Birmingham fittings, and patent everythings going of themselves everywhere; with, for all intellectual aids to felicity, a few bad prints, a few dirty and foolish books, and a quantity of photographs of the people they know, or of any passing celebrities.   This is the present ideal of English life, without exception, for the middle classes; and a more miserable, contemptible, or criminal one never was formed by any nation made under the wondering stars.   It implies perpetual anxiety, lazy and unjustifiable pride, innumerable petty vexations, daily more poignant greed for money, and the tyrannous compulsion of the labouring poor into every form of misery; and it implies, further, total ignorance of all the real honour of human life and beauty of the visible world.   I felt all this borne in upon me, almost to the point of making me give up all further effort here in England, and going away to die among the Alps, when I walked early this week across what were once fields, but are now platforms of mud and bitumen, to what we used to call the 'Happy Valley,' and the scenes, by Ferry Hinksey (but 'in the two Hinkseys nothing keeps the same'), of my former endeavours to set some undergraduates to useful country labour. [See *ante*, p. 45.] Every beautiful view, either of Oxford or from it, is now

scarified and blasted by the detestable conditions
of labour, which always mean that a company
or a capitalist are ruining either themselves or
somebody else. [Mr. Ruskin need not, though,
have put the alternative, for the Oxford Building Company has ruined both itself and many
others.] There is not an old path to be trodden,
or an old memory to be traced, except where
the discouraged and desperate cottagers here
and there maintain still a rugged fence or let
run a half-choked ditch round the melancholy
yards or gardens which they can still call their
own."

'Intelligent Destruction" of Birds.

"Now, what *is* the use," Mr. Ruskin went
on to ask, "under these conditions, of my talking to you about birds? Are their nests to be
built in the waterworks reservoir? is their song
to be heard in the morning above the steam
buzzer and the roll of the tramway? have you
still hearts to listen to it, if it could be? What
do you want of them now, but for such deadly
science or deadlier luxury as may best feed your
itch for notoriety of some sort—their skeletons
or their skins? And I have actually been un-
able, from the mere distress and disgust of what
I had to read of bird-slaughter, to go on with
'Love's Meinie.' I will make you a little miserable, with myself, in letting you hear accurately
described the sort of thing that is going on

continually." Mr. Ruskin then read two extracts from "a thoroughly trustworthy book,"
Mr. Robert Gray's "Birds of the West of Scotland," describing, among other things, how some
ornithologist of the party had shot two parent
divers and their little ones. Some others of the
party had seen the little ones the day before, and
had given them their first swimming lesson,
but the ornithologists wanted their skins. The
other extract told how the same party (minus
the ornithologists this time, it would seem) had
taken on board their yacht a live specimen of
the tysté, or black guillemot, and made a pet of
him. When he desired to leave his basket the
little fellow would "raise himself upon his hinder
end till he was almost as tall as a little spruce
tree; and then he would waddle on to the palm
of a person's hand, and sit there flapping his
wings as if he were flying at the rate of fifty
miles an hour; and then he would rest himself
on his abdomen, and shut one eye, and wink with
the other at the sun. But the cabin-boy said
from the beginning that he was too good to live.
The little creature died, I believe," Mr. Ruskin
here put in, "angelically, of being too happy;
but does not this show you how natural it is for
men and birds to love each other, and live with
each other joyfully?—if it were not for these
ghastly skin and bone mongers who call themselves ornithologists, and the still wretcheder
and ghastlier form of English booby squire, who
knows nothing and cares for nothing in all the
earth but how to wink along a gun-barrel till

he can sight it to blow the brains out of something, and he thinks that clever, and the best part of the life of a lord."

The Scientific View of Birds.

Mr. Ruskin then went on to illustrate, from a book of scientific travel, a different method of intelligent destruction—that of "the mob, who, not having guns, take to stones," and the kind of study of birds in connection therewith. Here is the method of destruction: "At one place ten cormorants and three steamer ducks were assembled on three small rocks, placed side by side, and would not take their departure till I had thrown a succession of stones at them. . . . One or two which had been hit with stones lay on their backs on the beach for some minutes, emitting strange sounds, and waving about their splay feet in the air, in the most ridiculous manner." And here is an example of what these sportsmen saw in a bird they had "fortunately killed:" "The stomach was distinctly divided into a cardiac and a pyloric portion, separated by a short and narrow interval. Of these portions the cardiac division possessed a comparatively feeble muscular coat, and was remarkably glandular; while the pyloric, of a somewhat flattened spheroidal form, was extremely muscular. The former I found distended with a firm mass of semi-digested ship biscuit, while the latter contained the two mandibles of a small cephalopod."

Birds in English Art.

This is the way English men of science look at birds, and English painters have hardly anything better to tell us of them. Art in this kind may be divided under four heads. There is first of all common still life—"dead game, with a cut lemon and a glass and bottle—the most wretched of human stupidities." Then there is still life, with some enjoyment of colour—"fruit pieces, usually with handsome plate—things such as Lance used to paint, and many other suppliers of the trade—not worth notice." Very different is William Hunt's work, whether in fruit or birds—"chiefly doves—unique in excellence, but still not didactic." And finally, there is the animal painting of Landseer and Mr. Briton Rivière. Landseer, however, is "strictly only a horse and dog painter; he seldom attempted birds, and when he did he failed. Rivière has done some wonderful ornithology—of a comic kind—as, for instance, in his 'An Anxious Moment,' in which a flock of geese are debating whether they may with safety pass by an old hat." *

The Artistic View of Birds; their Feathers.

The true portraiture of birds, then, is one of the things which English painters have still to

* See Appendix I., p. 210, for a reference to the birds of Mr. Stacy Marks.

do, and Mr. Ruskin's pupils would find plenty
of examples in his own studies in plumage in
his drawing-school.   But artists will never be
able to paint birds so long as they study in
modern schools of science.   " The true artist,"
Mr. Ruskin said, in a former Oxford lecture, "if
he wishes to paint a dog, looks at him and loves
him, does not vivisect him."   [See Appendix I.,
p. 206.]   So is it with birds.   Whatever Science
may be concerned with on its own account, as
a foundation for Art it must look at a bird's
plumage, not at the contents of its stomach.
Mr. Ruskin laid, therefore, some of this true
scientific groundwork on Saturday, by some
notes on feather analysis.   Birds, he said, have
three kinds of feathers : (1) feathers for clothing,
which again may be subdivided into flannel
feathers and armour feathers; (2) feathers for
action—either feathers of force in the wing, or
of steerage in the tail; and (3) feathers for
decoration and expression—which either modify
the bird's form (crests, *e.g.*, or tassels), or its
colour, by lustre or pigment.

Colours in Plumage.

It should be noted generally that the under-
clothing, the down, is always white in adult birds ;
and the prevailing colour of the upper feathers,
in land birds of temperate zones, brown, and in
sea birds white.   " The theorists of development," continued Mr. Ruskin, " say, I suppose,
that partridges get brown by looking at stubble,

seagulls white by looking at foam, and jackdaws black by looking at clergymen. The theory at first is plausible, as are the ideas of development in general, to people who like guessing better than thinking; but you may see its fallacy in an instant by reflecting that if sea birds were really coloured by the sea, they would be blue, not white; if land birds were coloured by their woods, they would be green, not brown; and that birds of darkness, both in feather and spirit, must have been suited with sable, not by our cathedral, but our manufacturing towns." Coming next to force feathers and decorative feathers, Mr. Ruskin noted that they are usually reserved and quiet in colour. "There is no iridescent eagle, no purple and golden seagull; while a large mass of coloured birds—parrots, pheasants, humming birds—seem meant for human amusement. Seem meant—dispute it if you will: no matter what they seem, they are the most amusing and infinitely delicious toys, lessons, comforts, amazements of human existence. Think of it, for here is a curious thing."

Catching Butterflies—and Feathers.

"Ever since I have known children," Mr. Ruskin said, in conclusion, "or heard talk of them, I have noticed that they liked running after butterflies, and are represented in poetical vignettes as if that were an amiable occupation of theirs. I would give any child I had the care of a good horsewhip or ponywhip cut over the

shoulders if I caught it running after a butterfly.
The way to see a butterfly is, as for everything
else, to see it alive. If you're quiet enough it
will settle under your nose or on your sleeve;
and if it's a rare one, and you don't kill it, it will
be less rare next year, until you may have purple
emperors flying about, as plentiful as now you
have smuts. But also when you've got it and
pinned it wriggling on a cork, what's the good
of it ? It is merely an ill-made bird, the inter-
mediate thing between a bird and a worm. It
has wings, but is for the most part more blown
about by them than lifted; it has legs, but it
can't hop with them or catch anything with
them; it has brains, but never has the least idea
where it's going; it has eyes, but doesn't see
anything particular with them that I know of;
ears, perhaps, I don't know; voice, I don't know;
anyhow, it can't whistle. Feathers it has, which
rub off if you touch them, like so much mildew.
A precious sort of thing to catch and transfix
what poor little life and succulent pleasure the
creature has evermore out of its body, that you
may pin it on your hat and say it's the Jackiana
Tomfooliensis ! But I will tell you what you
can catch, and catch innocently,—feathers; and
a single feather has more to study in it than fifty
butterflies. Here's Christmas coming—general
roast turkey and goose-pie time. You know I'm
no vegetarian. I wouldn't have you dine on
nightingales' tongues; but quantities of birds
are born, like sheep, to be finally dined on.
Well, you go and help the cook to pluck her

game, and in a single Christmas you may
gather plumage enough to be a wonder to you
all your days. Begin with the pheasant. Put
the characteristic breast, shoulder, wing, and
tail feather into explicable order, prettily stitched
down on cardboard, or velvet, or anything that
sets them off. Then put the feathers of any
other birds you can get hold of into the same
order—that is to say, put the main feather of
a seagull's wing, a swallow's, an owl's, a pheasant's, and a barn-door fowl's side by side—
similarly the main central types of breast
feather, tail feather, and so on. Then draw
their outlines carefully, then their patterns of
colour, then, analyzed up to the point of easy
magnifying, their shafts and filaments, and see
what a new world of beauty you will have
entered into—before the sun turns to go up
hill again."

" *Arise, my love, my fair one, and come
away.*"

"And when he does turn up hill again, if
any of you care to put your lives a little to
rights, and to prime your own feathers for what
flight is in them—don't go to London, nor to
any other town in the spring—don't let the
morning winds of May find your cheeks pale
and your eyes bloodshot with sitting up all
night, nor the violets bloom for you only in the
salesman's bundles, nor the birds sing around,
if not above, the graves you have dug for

yourselves before your time. Time enough you
will have hereafter to be deaf to their song,
and ages enough to be blind to their brightness,
if you seek not the sight given now. If there
be any human love in your youth, if any sacred
hope, if any faithful religion, let them not be
defiled and quenched among the iniquities of
the multitude. Your Love is in the clefts of
the Rock, when the flowers appear on the earth,
and the time of the singing of birds is come,
and the God of all Love calls to you 'from the
top of Amana, from the top of Shenir and
Hermon,' calls to every pure spirit among the
children of men, as they to those they love
best—

'Arise, my love, my fair one, and come away.'"

APPENDIX V.

A LECTURE ON LANDSCAPE.

(*Pall Mall Gazette*, December 10th, 1884. Mr. Ruskin
himself was good enough to subsequently revise
this report.)

MR. RUSKIN'S final lecture to his pupils for this
term, given at Oxford last week, began with an
expression of the " disappointment and surprise
which, on reviewing the results of my lecturing
and working here for upwards of twelve years,
I feel in being forced to the sorrowful confession
that not a single pupil has learned the things I
primarily endeavoured to teach, nor used of his
own accord, so far as I know, in a single instance, the examples which I put before him as
most admirable in my especial department of
art, landscape."

Examples of Landscape-drawing at Oxford.

How complete and numerous these examples
are every one knows who has visited the Taylorian picture-gallery or seen in the " Ruskin

Drawing-school" the insides of the cabinets filled with Mr. Ruskin's own drawings. "You may wonder," continued Mr. Ruskin, "why the examples I have given you of landscape in the school are my drawings and not Turner's. But Turner's are of a *finesse* beyond what has ever else been attained, and for that reason not useful as working examples. But I am proud to think that these drawings of mine" (several of which were exhibited at the lecture), "done thirty years ago at the foot of the Matterhorn, are entirely right as examples of mountain drawing, with absolutely correct outline of all that is useful for geological science or landscape art. And I am proud to think, too, that though at the time I did them I had never seen Turner's drawings, mine are on exactly the same plan as his—that is to say, I always drew an absolutely right pencil outline before putting in any colour whatever. But though I have been preaching, crying, shrieking to you that this is the method of all true landscape painting, there is not one of you who sharpens his pencil point, instead of seizing his biggest brush and going dab at the mountains with splashes of colour. And then in the gallery upstairs there is the unequalled collection of Turner drawings, which with some self-denial I gave you twenty years ago, and which has lately been completed by the kindness of the Trustees of the National Gallery, at the intercession of Prince Leopold."

Neglect of them by Mr. Ruskin's Pupils.

Why was it, then, Mr. Ruskin returned to ask, that none of his examples in landscape had been used, none of his principles adopted ? " I perhaps trusted too much to what I had before written on the subject of landscape, and in the first years of my professorship drew the attention of my pupils only to the higher conditions of pictorial imagination, which had been occupied in religion and ethics. As it has turned out, the religion of England being in its practical power extinct before her science, and the ethics of England extinct before her avarice, everything that I have written of the religious painting of Italy has been useless, until lately in the form of guide-books; while the value of the few words I spoke on landscape was still more hopelessly effaced by the vast irruption of sensual figure-study, patronized by the now all-powerful Republican *demi-monde* of the French capital. Respecting the general relations and dignities of landscape and figure-painting, I purpose very earnestly and carefully to address you in a spring lecture. But with respect to the especial danger and corruption of existing schools of the figure, I must point out one or two chief facts for your immediate consideration."

Landscape Superior to Figure Painting.

" First, landscape, however feeble or fantastic,

cannot be definitely immoral.   It neither mocks
what is venerable nor recommends what is
lascivious.   But the sale of figure sketches or
paintings, by persons of inferior talent, depends
almost exclusively on its being addressed to the
vanity, the lust, or the idle malice of the classes
of society developed by the corruption of large
towns.   Secondly, the idea of greater dignity
naturally attached to figure painting of higher
pretension, because it implies a strict course of
previous academical study, entirely ignores the
primary law of human education, that the more
you teach a fool the more manifold a fool you
make him.   Nothing is so melancholy, nothing
so mischievous, as the academical imitations of
the great men by the little ones, and the pompous
display of laboriously artificial attainments by
men of faculties inherently and natively contemptible.   During the first half of this century
the artists of England were divisible, almost
without exception, into two classes—men of
modesty, sense, and industry, who were forming
a pure school of pathetic and meditative landscape, rising with the quiet flow of a mountain
well out of the formality of the older 'views'
of this and that; and men, on the other hand,
of mean ambition, foolish sentiment, and vulgar
breeding, who reduced the figure-painting of
the Academy to the inanity from which it
was only rescued by the splendid indignation
of Rossetti, Millais, and Holman Hunt—all of
them, observe, introducing, if not as the basis,
at least as an essential and integral part of

their conception, a landscape elaborated to the last grass blade and flower petal."

Greater Difficulty of Landscape.

" Thirdly, I will not in this brief notice touch on the actual difficulties of landscape, as com-pared with figure painting, but I beg you to observe the requirement for it of far greater industry. With an hour's work a good figure painter can produce a satisfactorily realistic image of the fairest human creature ; set him to paint a heathy crag or a laurel coppice, and see what he will make of it, giving him an hour for every former minute, or sixty hours instead of one. Why, then, paint it with so much care, do you say, when the painting of the pretty lady is so much nicer ? Well, my own answer to that would be, Because the pretty lady herself is so much nicer than the painting, and will always be there if you ask her ; but the laurel coppice or the heather crag won't come for the asking ; you must paint them or forget them. Returning to my main point, note that the painting of landscape requires not only more industry, but far greater delicacy of bodily sense and faculty than average figure painting. Any common sign-painter can paint the land-lord's likeness, and with a year or two's scraping of chalk at Kensington any cockney student can be got to draw, effectively enough for public taste, a straddling gladiator or a curly-pated Adonis. But to give the slightest resemblance

to, or notion of, such a piece of mountain wild-
wood or falling stream as these, in this little
leap of the Tees in Turner's drawing, needs
an eagle's keenness of eye, fineness of finger
like a trained violinist's, and patience and love
like Griselda's or Lady Jane Grey's."

Delight in Landscape Dependent on Human Sympathy.

"Without, however, further reasoning just
now why or with what feelings we should try
to paint landscape, I return to my immediate
business, to ask you why in no single instance
any of you have painted a bit in my way. For
one of you that used to go to Scotland or Switzerland, a thousand go now; for one descriptive
passage in poetry or novel that used to be given
before Scott and Byron told you that nature
was beautiful, a thousand romancers and trou-
badours paint now their landscape backgrounds
for personages whom they couldn't make else of
any account; and yet here are twelve years I
have been your drawing-master, and not one of
you has brought me a bit of Alpine snow, of
Greek sea, or of English greenwood, drawn with
as much pains or heart as dear old William
Hunt put into a horn tankard. I do not know
what your answer would or will be. But my
own explanation of this scorn of landscape will
certainly surprise you. I attribute it, and I
attribute it with a very strong conviction, to

your having no sympathy with the people who inhabit the countries you visit. No passage of my old books is more often quoted than that in the 'Seven Lamps' as to the entire interest of landscape depending on our sympathy with its history and inhabitants." The passage in question is that in which Mr. Ruskin describes "the broken masses of pine forest which skirt the course of the Ain above the village of Champagnole, in the Jura," and which has been quoted above (see p. 17), as enforcing the dependence of landscape upon the human element for its power over the human heart. "But this point," Mr. Ruskin said, "I have never enough reinforced. The lecture in which I partly did so was never published; and you all go rushing about the world in search of Cotopaxis and Niagaras, when all the rocks of the Andes and all the river drainages of the two Americas are not worth to you, for real landscape, pathos, and power, this wayward tricklet of a Scottish burn over its shelves of low-levelled sandstone." Mr. Ruskin here showed the early Turner which he has lately acquired, and to which he referred, it will be remembered, in a former lecture. (See Appendix II., p. 255.) "Its whole force," he said, "consists in a dreamy and meditative sense that men were once living there, and that spirits are still moving there—that it was full of traces of the valour of our ancestors, just as it may still be full, if you will, of the sanctities of your love."

T

The Contrary Case, Illustrated from Evelyn's Diary.

To illustrate the contrary case—the absence of delight in landscape, accompanied and conditioned by a want of sympathy for the people —Mr. Ruskin read a series of extracts from Evelyn's Diary, written for him by his goddaughter with a type-writer—"the only kind of machine of which I do approve." First there was English enjoyment of English landscape at Spie Park, where the house had "not a window on the prospect side." That is the rough type; for the gentle type Mr. Ruskin referred to Evelyn's building a study, a fishpond, an island, and some other "solitudes and retirements" at Wotton, which "gave the first occasion of improving them to waterworks and gardens." As for English travellers' enjoyment of French landscape, "we passed through a forest (of Fontainebleau), so prodigiously encompassed with hideous rocks of white, hard stone, heaped one on another in mountainous height, that I think the like is nowhere to be found more horrid and solitary." For an example of "French and characteristically European manufactured landscape," Mr. Ruskin referred to Evelyn's description of Richelieu's villa, with its "walks of vast lengthes, so accurately kept and cultivated, that nothing can be more agreeable," and its "large and very rare grotto of shell-worke, in the shape of satyrs and other wild fancys." The human sympathy involved in manu-

factured landscape is to be seen in its cost—
" He has pulled downe a whole village to make
roome for his pleasure about it "—making a soli-
tude, and calling it delight. And then, lastly, Mr.
Ruskin read an account of how Evelyn took his
pleasure in the Alps, passing through " strange,
horrid, and fearful craggs," and treating the natives—as only the British tourist knows how.
The pious Evelyn, or one of his party, had a
water spaniel, "a huge, filthy cur," that killed
a goat, "whereupon we set spurrs and endeavoured to ride away;" but inasmuch as "amongst
these rude people a very small misdemeanour is
made much of, we lay'd down the money, though
the proceedings seemed highly unjust."   These
proceedings occurred on the Simplon Pass ; and
Mr. Ruskin showed, in contrast to them, a drawing of the St. Gothard, by Turner, in which,
as in other scenes, it is a human interest that
gives the grandeur.   The reader will remember
in this connection Mr. Ruskin's description of
the Pass of Faido, in " Modern Painters," where,
in "Turnerian typography," the "full essence
and soul of the scene and consummation of all
the wonderfulness of the torrents and Alps lay
in a postchaise with small ponies and postboy."
(See *ante*, p. 17.)

From the Alpine Club: Modern Manners.

"Now, I dare say," said Mr. Ruskin, resuming, "you all think you have improved greatly
in sense, and good-nature, and love of scenery

since Evelyn's time.   I admit there are a certain
number of you very different creatures indeed.
But there is nothing to me so amazing in Evelyn's
injustice to the poor peasants, and terrified hatred
of their Alps, as there is in the total absence
from the papers of the Alpine Club of the smallest expression of any human interest in anything
they see in Switzerland except the soaped poles
they want to get to the top of, and their continual
exultation, over their cheese and beer, in their
guides' legs and their own, without ever appearing conscious for an instant that every valley
of which the blue breaks through the cloud at
their feet is full of the most beautiful human
piety and courage, being gradually corrupted
and effaced by European vice, after contending
for long ages with conditions of hardship and
disease, prolonged by European neglect, folly,
and cruelty.   And of the less adventurous Eng-
lishman, content with flatter mountain tops, here
without question is the central type for this
hour."   Mr. Ruskin here showed *Punch's* cartoon of " The Old Lion Aroused," to which he
had referred in a former lecture, and in doing
so he apologized for any pain that had been
caused by his thus accidentally ridiculing Mr.
Bright—for whose character he had in most
things a great respect, although it was " an awful
sign of the times " that so honourable and excellent a man should have stood up on a memorable occasion in the House of Commons to
defend the adulteration of food as a legitimate
form of competition.   " You are all of you," Mr.

Ruskin resumed, with reference to this cartoon, "resolving yourselves, and that with rapidity, into this kind of British person, and this kind of British standard-bearer—consumer of all things consumable, producer of nothing but darkness and abomination, with his foot on all that he once revered, his hope lost in all that he once worshipped, a god to himself, and to all the world an incarnate calamity."

The Return to Nature.

"Your way out of all this I told you full fourteen years ago, in my inaugural lectures, to not one word of which any of you have practically attended. I have, indeed, one pupil-friend, an accomplished and amiable artist, another a conscientious and prosperous lawyer—of formal school or consistent disciples no vestige whatever. The time may yet come; anyhow next year I have again, with the ever-ready help of Mr. Macdonald, to begin at the beginning, and meanwhile I will close my discourses to you for this year by re-reading the conditions of prosperous art work which I laid before you in 1870." The passage which Mr. Ruskin read is in the fourth of his inaugural "Lectures on Art," on "The Relation of Art to Use," in which it was laid down that after recovering, for the poor, wholesomeness of food, the next steps towards founding Schools of Art in England must be in recovering for them decency and wholesomeness of dress and of lodging, and

then after this that " nothing be ever made of
iron that can be as effectually made of wood or
stone, and nothing moved by steam that can be
as effectually moved by natural forces. . . . And
until you do this, be it soon or late, things will
continue in that triumphant state to which, for
want of finer art, your mechanism has brought
them; that though England is deafened with
spinning-wheels, her people have not clothes;
though she is black with digging of fuel, they
die of cold; and though she has sold her soul
for gain, they die of hunger.   Stay in that
triumph, if you choose; but be assured of this,
it is not one which the Fine Arts will ever share
with you."

"All this," said Mr. Ruskin, in conclusion,
"is called impossible.   It may be so.   I have
nothing to do with its possibility, but only with
its indispensability.   And at any rate this much
is possible to you—to prefer life in the country,
though it be dull, to life in London, though it is
merry; to look at one thing in the day, instead
of at twenty; and to think of that one in such
a way as will give you some love for man and
some belief in God."

INDEX.

THE END.

PRINTED BY BALLANTYNE, HANSON AND CO.
EDINBURGH AND LONDON.